In 2 Timothy, God has provid
and standard of ministry fo
corrects our assumptions and
many popular current theorie:
ministry. It challenges and enco
us to do, warns us of dangers, a.... ...veals the God-given goals
and means we should follow.

This book by Jonathan Griffiths is a brilliantly effective study,
which makes good use of 2 Timothy to give us a diagnostic
tool to assess the health of our ministry. It would be equally
productive for those starting out in ministry, those in their
middle years, and those nearing the finishing line! It is simple
and straightforward: the format of questions and comments
works very well, and makes the book very user-friendly. This
book will help you fight the good fight, finish the race, and keep
the faith. Highly recommended.

Peter Adam
Former Principal of Ridley College, Melbourne and Vicar Emeritus of
St. Jude's, Carlton, Melbourne, Australia

I thoroughly recommend taking *The Ministry Medical.* Because
the questions are taken straight from 2 Timothy, here is God's
check-up for any minister of the gospel today. These 36
brilliantly concise chapters call us back to the essential priorities
of truly Christian ministry. This will be a book to take down
from the shelf again and again, to pray through and to share
with colleagues and lay leaders.

Alistair Paine
Vicar of St Andrew the Great and Trustee of Keswick Ministries
Cambridge, England

Paul's Second Letter to Timothy, along with the other Pastoral
Epistles, is the God-given blueprint for a faithful biblical
ministry. Jonathan Griffiths's superb book is a wonderful vehicle
for allowing 2 Timothy to search us out, rebuke us, reshape us
and encourage us on in gospel work. This is a health-check every

servant of the Word will want to undergo·– whether starting out in ministry, continuing in the mid years or pushing for the finishing line. It will benefit every gospel minister and can be used in quiet times or for group study within an eldership or a staff team.

Greg Strain
Senior Pastor, Spicer Street Church
St Albans, England

This wonderful book distils Paul's second letter to Timothy into 36 simple, searching and strategic questions for all who are seeking to preach the Word. Written with clarity and honesty, *The Ministry Medical* is practical and personal, reflective and refreshing. The book calls us back to the Apostolic shape of life and ministry, to the hard work of living for and proclaiming Jesus Christ. It is a magnificent resource and reminder for all in pastoral ministry and I highly recommend it.

David Short
Rector of St. John's and member of the Council of the Gospel Coalition
Vancouver, Canada

THE MINISTRY MEDICAL

A Health-check from 2 Timothy

Jonathan Griffiths

PT RESOURCES

CHRISTIAN
FOCUS

Jonathan Griffiths is married to Gemma and they have two young children. Jonathan holds a PhD in New Testament studies from the University of Cambridge and was editor of *The Perfect Saviour: Key themes in Hebrews* (IVP, 2012). He served as assistant minister at Christ Church, Westbourne before joining the staff of the PT Cornhill Training Course.

Copyright © Jonathan Griffiths

paperback ISBN 978-1-78191-232-4
epub ISBN 978-1-78191-261-4
Mobi ISBN 978-1-78191-262-1

10 9 8 7 6 5 4 3 2 1

Published in 2013
by
Christian Focus Publications,
Geanies House, Fearn, Ross-shire,
IV20 1TW, Scotland, Great Britain
with
Proclamation Trust Resources,
Willcox House, 140-148 Borough High Street,
London, SE1 1LB, England, Great Britain.
www.proctrust.org.uk

www.christianfocus.com

Cover design by
Daniel van Straaten

Printed by
Bell and Bain, Glasgow

Contents

Acknowledgements

I have used a limited number of commentaries in writing this short book, and these are listed in the Bibliography. Although I would not follow each one at every point, I happily commend all those listed as useful resources for studying and preaching 2 Timothy. Of the commentaries mentioned, I have made more intensive use of the works by Kelly, Stott and Green. Readers familiar with their books will see my debt to them, and I gratefully acknowledge it here. Two further resources have been of particular help to me: the talks given by Peter Adam at the 2001 *Senior Ministers' Conference* and those given by Dick Lucas for the 1986 *Evangelical Ministry Assembly* (both conferences of the *Proclamation Trust*). Both series are packed full of biblical insight and pastoral wisdom born of many years of ministry experience, and both are available through the *Proclamation Trust* via www.proctrust.org.uk.[1]

I have been grateful for the opportunity to preach through much of 2 Timothy at Christ Church, Westbourne and to teach through 2 Timothy at the PT Cornhill Training Course. Much

---

1   References to Peter Adam and Dick Lucas throughout this book refer to these two series of talks.

of the material here has been 'road-tested' and received with a gracious and patient hearing in both contexts, and I am very thankful for the constructive feedback I have received.

This book has been much improved through the wise counsel of Dick Lucas, Adrian Reynolds, David Jackman and my grandfather, Gerald Griffiths. I am much indebted to them for their kindness in reading the manuscript and for the feedback and encouragement they have given. I am also thankful for the proofreading labours of Beckie Hollands and Lisa Williamson in the Proclamation Trust office, and for the editorial work of Kate MacKenzie and the rest of the Christian Focus team.

Like all my work in ministry, this project has only really been possible because of the patient help and encouragement of my wife, Gemma. It is dedicated to her with love.

A few words of introduction

The book of 2 Timothy sets out the authoritative pattern for gospel ministry in the post-apostolic age. It is therefore a letter that gospel ministers should return to regularly and consider carefully. It acts as a plumb-line to re-align our ministry and a health-check to measure its vitality. What are the marks of a healthy gospel ministry that endures and bears fruit? What are the characteristics to aim for and the pitfalls to avoid? How do I know if I am getting it right in my own ministry?

This is Paul's final letter. He writes from a Roman prison, conscious that death is imminent and his ministry is drawing to a close (4:6-8). More than that, Paul sees the big picture: he stands near the close of the apostolic era, aware that very soon gospel ministry will be entirely in the hands of next generation leaders like Timothy. So Paul writes to him to urge him to guard the deposit of the apostolic teaching (1:14) through fearlessly preaching the apostolic Word (4:2). Alongside his explicit instruction to Timothy, Paul sets out his own pattern of life and ministry as a model for Timothy to follow. Again and again in the letter, Paul *tells* Timothy how he should live and minister and then *shows* Timothy how he himself has lived out the pattern he describes.

The Ministry Medical

Paul had left Timothy in Ephesus to 'command certain men not to teach false doctrines any longer nor to devote themselves to myths and endless genealogies. These promote controversies rather than God's work—which is by faith' (1 Tim. 1:3-5). Sure enough, Timothy had found plenty of false teaching circulating in Ephesus. False teachers like Hymenaeus and Philetus had '... wandered away from the truth. They say that the resurrection has already taken place ...' (2 Tim. 2:17-18). Such a message, implying that all God's future promises are fulfilled in the here and now, would have been music to the ears of the cosmopolitan population of Ephesus, a prosperous trade hub with all the trappings and enticements of wealth. Paul is convinced that only worse is to come and that Timothy will soon find that people simply will not put up with hearing the true gospel (4:3).

Here the great apostle lays out for his trusted protégé, through instruction and personal model, a definitive pattern for faithful ministry in the post-apostolic age. His aim in this letter is to ensure that the work of gospel proclamation continues uncompromised from the close of the apostolic era until the appearing of Jesus.

Paul's instructions and personal model for faithful ministry remain the standard for every generation. They were written to Timothy in the first instance, but they are very much for us pastor-teachers today. The aim of this short book is simply to boil down the instructions Paul gives, and the characteristics of his own ministry that he commends, so that we may see how our own lives and ministries measure up. Each of these instructions and characteristics has been turned into a question to help us apply it personally and consider its implications for ourselves.

The book of 2 Timothy is written to a pastor-teacher in the cut and thrust of real-life ministry, and this book has as its primary audience pastor-teachers in the midst of their ministry. More specifically, 2 Timothy is written to a younger pastor-teacher still in the early years of his ministry. As a younger

A few words of introduction

pastor-teacher myself, I have found 2 Timothy to be just the book I need to show me what good ministry looks like and to model for me what I should prayerfully aspire to become. It shows up some of the particular temptations and blind spots of the younger minister, and I have found that I have been repeatedly rebuked and corrected as I have studied this letter. So I would particularly commend this 'health-check' to the younger minister. I trust as well that these 36 questions drawn from 2 Timothy will be a challenge, prompt and refresher for any pastor-teacher at any stage in his ministry. Doubtless, pastor-teachers with more experience in ministry will draw from their experience many applications and implications of what Paul wrote to Timothy that have not yet occurred to me.

There are a number of others who I hope will also be able to read this book with benefit. If you are not a pastor-teacher but you still exercise some form of Christian leadership through Word ministry (as a home group leader, or Sunday school teacher, or summer camp leader), I hope that there will be much here to challenge and encourage you. At some points in the book I have highlighted ways in which the principles of 2 Timothy will apply particularly to you, but I have not done that throughout. So, if you fall into that bracket, do please read on, but read discerningly, knowing that some principles here will be less directly applicable to you.

If you are considering Word ministry for the future and are perhaps training for Word ministry at the moment, the questions here are relevant for you, but the tense simply needs to be changed. Rather than asking, 'Am I doing these things?', you simply need to ask, '*Can* I and *will* I do these things?' I hope you will go through this list and ask the questions. It may well be that you will look at the list and think: 'This simply is not for me!' That in itself would be useful; better to find that out now rather than in ten years' time. If, on the other hand, giving thought to the model of ministry outlined in 2 Timothy gives you a fresh sense of the magnitude of the task and leads you to further humility and prayerful dependence on God for his help as you move forward, that would be of great value too.

Finally, if you are a praying member of a local church (and that should be all of us!), then this book has value for you too: it will show you what biblically-faithful ministry looks like and what kinds of pressures your pastor will face, and it will help you to pray for him and encourage him in his ministry.

To set realistic expectations, I should say at the outset that this is not designed to be an exhaustive study guide or, even less, a full exposition of 2 Timothy. Much of what Paul says in his letter is not dealt with here. This is a selective treatment designed as a diagnostic to help us to think about specific aspects of our own ministry. Exegetical decisions are largely kept in the background and are not defended in any detail.

I would suggest considering the questions outlined in this book slowly and over a period of a number of weeks. Probably the most fruitful way to use this book is to read it alongside reading 2 Timothy in your personal Bible reading time, ideally over 36 days. Another useful approach would be to read it with a group of other leaders, perhaps with your ministry staff or elders during your regular meetings over a period of a few months, taking one or two questions at a time and then considering and praying through their application to you and your church. Paul tells Timothy to allow himself time to digest what he says in this letter, and we would do well to heed his instruction: 'Reflect on what I am saying, for the Lord will give you insight into all this' (2:7).

A few words of encouragement

The pattern of ministry that Paul outlines for Timothy and for us in his letter is, in many ways, quite daunting. I have found it sobering and humbling to reflect on it and to set my ministry against it, and I imagine you will too. However, 2 Timothy is not here to drive us to despair. Like all Scripture, it is here so that we may be 'thoroughly equipped for every good work' (2 Tim. 3:17). With that in mind, I want to begin with the encouragement that Paul gives us in his opening chapter that the gospel itself makes ministry both thoroughly possible and immensely worthwhile. Notice how Paul frames his initial call to Timothy to suffer alongside him in ministry:

> So do not be ashamed to testify about our Lord, or ashamed of me his prisoner. But join with me in suffering for the gospel, by the power of God, who has saved us and called us to a holy life—not because of anything we have done but because of his own purpose and grace. This grace was given us in Christ Jesus before the beginning of time, but it has now been revealed through the appearing of our Saviour, Christ Jesus, who has destroyed death and has brought life and immortality to light through the

gospel. And of this gospel I was appointed a herald and an apostle and a teacher. That is why I am suffering as I am. Yet I am not ashamed, because I know whom I have believed, and am convinced that he is able to guard what I have entrusted to him for that day. (1:8-12)

First, be encouraged that the gospel makes ministry *possible*. We must remember that our service is only made possible because God has called us into His family 'not because of our works but because of his own purpose and grace'. We are what we are only because God has set us apart through His sheer kindness and mercy. And we are what we are only because, in His grace, God has removed our guilt at the cross and given us what we could never earn or deserve, the righteousness of Jesus. We are only fit to serve because God has included us 'in Christ Jesus' and made us His very own holy people. Our ministry does not rest on our merits, but solely on the merits of Jesus, and our power to share in the suffering involved in ministry comes from God Himself ('... by the power of God ...'), who fills us with his Spirit and equips us day-by-day. Although we are powerless in ourselves, God through the gospel has made it possible for us to serve as ministers of the gospel.

More than that, God makes it possible for us to continue in ministry despite our sin and failures and shortcomings. In 2 Timothy Paul will set out for Timothy and for us a standard in ministry that we will never attain to perfectly and completely. Presumably Paul is writing this letter to Timothy, who already knows so much of the theory of ministry (he has already been given 1 Timothy), because he is a sinner who needs constant encouragement to minister faithfully. Our ministries will never be marked by sinless perfection this side of heaven. That is why Paul begins, not with instruction, but with gospel-grace: 'To Timothy, my dear son: *Grace, mercy and peace from God the Father and Christ Jesus our Lord.*' (1:2) Paul's awareness of Timothy's need for grace and encouragement is surely part of the reason why Paul gives so much attention to the gospel itself in his first chapter. Whatever our congregation might think of us, and whatever we might expect of ourselves, we do not suddenly cease to be sinners when we enter full-time ministry. We constantly need to receive God's mercy and grace that we might know and enjoy his peace. God through the gospel has made it possible for us to serve, and makes it possible for us to *keep on serving*, as ministers of the gospel.

Second, be encouraged that the gospel makes ministry *worthwhile*. It is helpful for us, at regular intervals, to clear away all the mental clutter of our day – church administration to do and emails to answer and talks to write – and to go back to basics for a few quiet moments and ask: 'Why am I a Christian?' 'Why does the gospel matter?' 'Why did I choose to go into full-time ministry in the first place?' 'What motivated me then?'

When we ask these questions we quickly get back to the fundamental issues of life and death. The problem of death and the promise of life must lie at the heart of our understanding of the gospel and our motivation in ministry because they lie at the heart of the Bible's salvation storyline. The tree of life was what God barred to us in the Garden and death was the sentence God placed on us for sin. The fear of death is the great enemy that enslaves the world (Heb. 2:15), but Jesus offers life to all who will believe (John 3:16). There are seasons in our lives and ministries when the full horror of death comes home to us sharply, but we need regularly to remind ourselves of it.

I write these words days after another school massacre in the United States, this one claiming the lives of twenty small children and six adults. Suddenly it is as though the world collectively feels the sting of death again. And feeling that sting alongside everyone else, the words of 2 Timothy 1:10 thrill me afresh: Jesus has 'destroyed death and has brought life and immortality to light through the gospel'. As gospel people and gospel ministers, you and I have the privilege of proclaiming to a grieving and fearful world that Jesus has abolished the great enemy that is death and opened up the way to life and immortality. For those who will trust Him, there is the sure promise of life.

Now, tell me, what better work is there than proclaiming the abolition of death and inviting a dying world to live? It is no surprise that Paul says that his appointment to proclaim this message is sufficient reason to 'suffer as I do'. Be encouraged. To labour and even suffer for such a gospel is immensely worthwhile.

1

Are you praying for your people?

> I thank God...as night and day I constantly
> remember you in my prayers.... (1:3)

It is often said that the quickest way to embarrass a Christian is to ask him about his prayer life, and many of us in ministry will feel that sense of embarrassment particularly acutely. We know that the work to which we must devote ourselves is 'prayer and the ministry of the word' (Acts 6:4), but because our study of the Word is such labour-intensive work (and because it is so obvious when we fail to give time to it), prayer often loses out. Well, here is a gentle encouragement from the example of the apostle Paul to put praying back at the top of our agenda.

Paul was a great pray-er, and his prayer life overflows into his letters time and time again. Prayer was the great secret behind the effectiveness of his discipleship of young leaders like Timothy. Paul loved Timothy as a son and made no secret of it: 'I long to see you, so that I may be filled with joy' (1:4). But this was no idle sentimentality; Paul's heartfelt affection and concern for Timothy and his ministry was channelled, not only into teaching him and corresponding with him, but into daily prayer. This prayer was full of thanksgiving for the evidence of God's gracious work in Timothy's life and ministry ('I thank God....'). We can be quite sure that each of the admonitions and instructions contained in this letter had first been the subject of much intercessory prayer for Timothy that God would strengthen and equip him for the work before him.

Paul's personal model provides a threefold challenge for us in our prayer life. First, are we praying for our people regularly – 'constantly', 'night and day'? We all have our own systems and patterns for praying and we will all do this (or, at least aim to do this!) in different ways. But to be faithful in 'constant' prayer for our people will require two types of habit in the life of the minister. It will almost certainly require us to follow some sort of list or plan for praying for each of our people by name. In my last church, we had a prayer directory that simply took the membership list and divided it into 29 parts, and so I aimed to pray for a handful of people each day and for the whole church family over the course of every month. That works if you have a church of 50 or 100 or even 200. It is less easy, and eventually impossible, if you are ministering to a much larger congregation. Perhaps you can only pray for your people by name every few months. If that is the case, it would be worth identifying a core group to whom you minister more intensively – your elders and their families, your staff team, or your home group – and pray for them more regularly. Alongside planned praying for our people, the habit of 'constant' prayer will also mean praying spontaneously and as a matter of reflex for people as we minister to them day by day. When people appear on our doorstep in crisis, praying with them and for them should be our first response. When we prepare to teach the Bible to our people, we must be praying for God to do his mighty work in their hearts as they listen to his Word. When we head off to the hospital to visit a dying saint, the visit should be preceded by prayer, filled with prayer, and followed by prayer. It all sounds very obvious, but how easily prayer is squeezed out in the busyness of ministry. Are we those who pray 'constantly', 'night and day' for our people?

Are you praying for your people?

Second, are we giving thanks for God's work in our people? It is so easy in the work of ministry to see the problems and disappointments. People seem to lack hunger for God's Word; they appear to be unconcerned about their own godliness; they lack motivation for evangelism; they seem unwilling to serve – and then there is the matter of our own half-heartedness! But if the Spirit of God is at work by his Word in our church family, there will be life and progress and growth. There will always be encouragements mixed in with the discouragements. And those signs of life and progress are wonderful evidences of the gracious work of God in our midst. We plead for God to bring a person to new life, to turn him from sin, to equip her for service – but how often we fail to give him thanks when He graciously answers our prayers. Where has God been at work recently in the lives of your people? Are you giving thanks to him?

Third, are we praying for our people before we teach and admonish them? It is telling how frequently Paul precedes his instruction by prayer (Rom. 1:8-10; 1 Cor. 1:4-7; Eph. 1:15-23; Phil. 1:3-5; Col. 1:3, 9-14; 1 Thess. 1:2-3; Philem. 4-6). Paul knew that if any spiritual work was to be accomplished in the people under his care, God himself would have to do it by the power of his Spirit. At a church where my wife and I were members some years ago, the senior minister used to remind us of the vital importance of the prayer meeting each month by recounting this basic truism: 'When we work, *we* work; when we pray, *God* works.' We can work and teach all we want – with all 'blood, toil, tears and sweat', to borrow a Churchillian phrase – but if we are not prayerfully waiting upon the Lord to work, we should expect no fruit. Is our preparation for sermons and Bible studies and personal work and hospital visiting covered in humble and dependent prayer? Or have we become proud and self-sufficient, imagining that the power to change people rests with us?

If, like me, you sense the inadequacy of your own prayer life, take Paul's model of prayer-filled ministry as a prompt and encouragement to make more of the privilege of prayer. Even Paul the great apostle knew that he needed prayerfully to rely on God's power for all he undertook to do, and he knew that he needed to give God the praise for any fruit he saw.

2

Are you serving with a clear conscience?

> I thank God, whom I serve, as my forefathers
> did, with a clear conscience, as night and day
> I constantly remember you in my prayers. (1:3)

The book of 2 Timothy is very much Paul's 'last will and testament to the church'.[1] He knows that his ministry is drawing to a close and that his death is near (4:6), and he now looks back on his ministry as a fight fought and a race run (4:7). As Paul looks back, he tells us here that he does so with a 'clear conscience'.

Paul is not saying this because he is given to introspection and certainly not because he is inclined to self-congratulation. The personal reflections on his own ministry here in 2 Timothy are given for Timothy's good. Paul is keenly aware that the stewardship of the gospel and the care of God's people is passing from him to Timothy and young men like him. Paul wants Timothy to learn all he can from his own model of ministry.

For Paul, the state of his conscience as a gospel minister is hugely important. He knows the seriousness of his work and

---

1.   Stott, *2 Timothy*, p. 18.

the sobering reality of his ultimate accountability to the Lord for his faithfulness in it. He knows that letting go of 'a good conscience' is a sure way to wander into false teaching and ungodliness (see 1 Tim. 1:6-11, 18-20; 4:1-5). For Paul, keeping a good conscience in his life and ministry involves godly living, diligence in carrying out the ministry he has been given, faithfulness to the truth, and boldness in proclaiming it (see also 1 Cor. 4:4).

When Paul leaves the region of Ephesus in Acts 20 and addresses the Ephesian elders, he tells them why it is that he closes his ministry in that place with a clear conscience: 'Therefore, I declare to you today that I am innocent of the blood of all men. For I have not hesitated to proclaim to you the whole will of God' (Acts 20:26-27). Paul knows that he will not approach Jesus the Judge on the final day with blood on his hands because he has declared to the people of Ephesus the fullness of God's Word. He has not been selective; he has not left out the hard or unpalatable elements of it; he has spoken the truth and the whole truth.

Consider for a moment the flip-side of what Paul is saying to the Ephesian elders. Presumably Paul means that, had he shrunk back from speaking the whole counsel of God – had he gone quiet on the fact of God's judgment, or the nature of God's requirements for his people's holiness in a worldly place like Ephesus, or the uniqueness of Jesus in a pluralistic place like Ephesus, he would then approach the judgment with blood on his hands. He would have blood on his hands because there would be people from Ephesus in grave danger on that final day because Paul had been too cowardly or too lazy to warn them.

The writer of Hebrews makes a similar connection in chapter 13 of his letter. He urges the congregation to 'obey your leaders and submit to their authority. They keep watch over you as men who must give an account' (13:17). The writer, who is a leader of the congregation (and hopes to return to them soon, v. 19), says that he has a 'clear conscience and desire[s] to live honourably in every way' (v. 18). The writer of Hebrews is another example of a Christian leader declaring the whole counsel of God to his people and so discharging faithfully his duty before God. In his letter he speaks clearly of the whole of God's salvation plan, including the warning of judgment for those who reject the gospel.

Christian leaders need to minister with a clear conscience. Our lifestyle needs to be marked by holiness (more on that to come), and our teaching needs to be marked with bold faithfulness because we ourselves will give account to Jesus the Judge for the souls under our care.

How is your conscience? It may well be that you look back at particular occasions where you have failed to declare the full counsel of God and you regret it very much. All of us will look back on situations in ministry that we have not handled with the grace, godliness, boldness or faithfulness that we should have. Here is the good news: there is grace for the sinner – even the sinful and compromised gospel minister. And so we can go forward with a cleansed conscience and with the merits of Jesus accounted to us. But as we rejoice in that good news, let us also resolve, with God's help, to minister with a clear conscience as we press on.

3

Are you fanning into flame the gift of God?

> ...I remind you to *fan into flame the gift of God*, which
> is in you through the laying on of my hands... (1:6)

Timothy had received a gift from the Lord for Word ministry.
That much is clear from Paul's recollection of his ordination in
1 Timothy 4:13-16 and his instruction to Timothy to proclaim
the Word in 2 Timothy 4:1. What is interesting here is that
Paul needs to remind Timothy to fan this gift 'into flame'. This
exhortation reminds us that the natural tendency of the gift
of Word ministry (placed as it is in the life of a sinful person)
is to dwindle and burn out. If it is not fed and stoked and
encouraged – if as a fire it is left untended – it will dwindle and
even disappear. The warmth and light and power will fade away.
Simply possessing the gift of Word ministry does not mean
that the gift will be automatically operative; we may have the
gift, but if we are not working hard at fanning it into flame, our
ministry will not bear the marks of the gifts God has given us,
and it will be lifeless.

What will it look like to 'fan into flame' the gift of Word
ministry? Presumably it will mean continuing to work hard
at our Bible understanding and Bible handling; continuing to

work hard at knowing our people and our culture so that our applications and exhortations will hit home; and continuing to work hard at prayer, humbly asking the Lord to help us and so make his word effective for our hearers.

One of the things that struck me when I first started out in ministry was just how hard it was to prepare a sermon. I reckon some of my early sermons took as much as 50 hours to write. But I comforted myself by assuring myself that it would get easier as time went on. What I actually discovered was that, although I got a bit faster at putting a sermon together, the work did not actually get any *easier*. It is labour, sheer hard work, studying the Bible and getting it right and then reading the surrounding culture and knowing the congregation well enough to preach the Word to them in a powerful and life-transforming way.

Although Word ministry never gets easy, I think we can reach a stage (and others further on in Word ministry than me attest to this) when we start to fake it; we become good enough at making it look like we have done the hard work on the text so that our congregation thinks we have actually put in the hard slog. That is a dangerous stage to reach because our temptation will always be to take the route of least resistance and simply fake it – to stop working at the text and to stop working at our preaching. I take it that that is just the kind of thing that Paul is telling Timothy *not* to be doing when he says 'fan into flame the gift of God'.

One practical way to keep ourselves working at the text and to keep us honest about the work we are doing is to establish a preaching group in our local area or, if we are part of a preaching team, within our church. In that way we could spend time with fellow preachers talking about our preparation and work on the text, thinking through sermon structure, illustrations and applications, and then giving each other feedback on how it went. In that kind of context we will be challenged to keep growing and will find it difficult to hide if we are not doing the hard work.

Are you fanning into flame the gift of God?

For Timothy, the charge to work hard at his preaching gift was an urgent one. Remember the big picture: Paul's apostolic ministry was drawing to a close (4:6), and he knew that the future spread of the gospel and protection of the church rested on Timothy and younger ministers like him faithfully proclaiming the truth. Those younger ministers urgently needed to work hard at their gift and not grow lazy for fear that their ministry gift should burn out and the Word fail to go out.

The urgency is undiminished in our day.

Are you fanning into flame your gift for Word ministry? If not, what steps can you take to discipline yourself to do so, and to keep doing so, for the long haul?

4

Are you serving in the power of the Spirit?

> For this reason I remind you to fan into flame the
> gift of God, which is in you through the laying on
> of my hands. For God did not give us a spirit of
> timidity, but a spirit of power, of love and of self-
> discipline. So do not be ashamed to testify about
> our Lord, or ashamed of me his prisoner. But join
> with me in suffering for the gospel, by the power
> of God.... (1:6-8)

I don't know what you might expect a Spirit-filled ministry
to look like. Perhaps in your mind it looks like a ministry that
draws crowds, or is particularly innovative, or has a prophetic
cutting-edge. It is both striking and instructive to see the vital
role of the Spirit here in Timothy's ministry according to
Paul. The apostle has just reminded Timothy to work hard at
developing and maintaining his preaching gift. That is going to
require serious effort. But Timothy should not despair because,
like all other believers and like Paul himself, he has received the
Holy Spirit, who will help him. This Spirit and his work in the
life of the believer is characterised not by 'fear', but by 'power',
'love' and 'self-control'. Given that Timothy has such a Spirit to

empower his preaching ministry, he should proclaim the gospel unashamedly, and share in the suffering that will result.

Far from being impressive and necessarily 'successful' in the world's estimation, a Spirit-filled ministry is a ministry that will work hard at the preaching of the gospel and be willing to suffer for the gospel unashamedly.

It is worth noting here the coupling of necessary human effort ('I remind you to fan into flame...', v. 6) and the Spirit's enabling ('... for God gave us a Spirit....', v. 7, ESV).[1] The two go hand-in-hand. We cannot be effective or survive in gospel ministry without the Spirit's enabling and empowering. But there is no promise of the Spirit's enabling of lazy ministry where there is no human effort. The gifts of ministry are not automatically operative. The Spirit empowers the minister who works hard. It's not a choice between hard work or the Spirit's enabling; both must go together.

Let's think for a moment about the three characteristics of the Holy Spirit and his work in the life of a gospel minister. First, He is a Spirit of 'power'. Gospel ministry takes stamina. Those in local church ministry know how relentless is its pace and infinite its scope. We labour to present everyone under our care to the Lord at the final day 'perfect in Christ' (Col. 1:28). It takes time and hard work and persevering prayer. Until this goal is reached, the work is never done. There is always another sermon to prepare, always more people to pray for, always more people to read the Bible with, always more home visits to do, and on and on it goes. So, what a good thing it is that the Spirit we have is a Spirit who gives power to the weak. Paul knew what he was talking about here; he is the same Paul who suffered a painful and unrelenting physical affliction that taught him the vital lesson that the Lord's 'power is made perfect in weakness' (2 Cor. 12:9).

However, the power required in ministry is not simply the power to give stamina, but the power to proclaim the truth boldly

---

1. The NIV and ESV read 'spirit' rather than 'Spirit' in verse 7. This is a debated point, but it seems most natural to me to see here a reference to the Holy Spirit given to Paul, Timothy and all believers ('us'), rather than a reference to a particular demeanour in ministry ('a spirit') that God gives to the pastor-teacher.

and make the Word hit home in the hearts and minds of our hearers. Remember what Paul said the Spirit was not like: He is not a Spirit who produces 'fear'. I take it that we will always be tempted to cowardice when it comes to proclaiming the truth of God's Word in its fullness because it will be offensive to our hearers. But the Spirit God has given us is the Spirit who gives us courage and boldness to say the hard things and to bear the scorn and anger of our hearers who find it all too much to stomach. More than that, the Holy Spirit makes our weak preaching and teaching powerful as He drives it home to the hearts and minds of our hearers. The very message that we may feel is weak, poorly constructed and feebly delivered is so often made surprisingly powerful for our hearers, and that is a mark of the Spirit's gracious work. John Stott said that he rarely stepped down from the pulpit at All Soul's without repenting of his feeble preaching, but how powerful the Holy Spirit made John Stott's weakness as his words travelled to the ears and hearts of thousands whose lives were changed under his preaching ministry.

The Holy Spirit is, next, a Spirit of love. He is the same Spirit who has poured out the redeeming love of God in our own hearts, showing us that God, who is rightly opposed to us because of our sin, has reconciled us to Himself through the costly sacrifice of his Son. The Spirit who taught us that God loves us is the same Spirit who enables us to love the people to whom we minister. Sometimes it is very easy to love the people we serve in ministry. Sometimes they will be responsive to our preaching and teaching and full of gratitude for our labours. But sometimes, as we all know, our hearers will be unresponsive or worse, and we will find it hard to love them. Wonderfully, though, the Spirit teaches and enables us to love them, and loving them, He teaches us to work hard at faithful Bible proclamation for the sake of their spiritual good. It is a *loving* thing to preach the Word faithfully and to be willing to suffer for it, because our hearers need the Word in its fullness so that they may know and trust the Saviour. It is unloving for us not to fan into flame the gift of God, because if our preaching is not faithful and not of a high standard – if our gift is burning down to an ember –

our congregation will struggle to listen to the Word and that will do them no spiritual good.

Finally, the Spirit we have been given is a Spirit of self-discipline. Keeping going in faithful Word ministry requires self-discipline in every area of life. Much of the work done (or, not done) in Word ministry is done alone, in the study and without outside observers. It takes self-discipline to use that time effectively and not to fritter it away. If we tend toward laziness, it takes self-control really to be working when no one is looking. On the other end of the spectrum, if we tend toward over-work, it takes self-discipline to set limits around work, because the nature of the task is such that it is never finished. In situations where we face opposition, it takes self-discipline ('self-control', ESV) not to lose our temper and not to lose our focus on the task ahead of us. When we find people within the church family difficult, it takes self-control not to lose patience with them. All this is beyond us, but thank the Lord for his Spirit, who gives self-discipline to those who naturally lack it.

Peter Adam notes how dangerous it would be to have a ministry marked by only two out of the three characteristics of Spirit-filled ministry. Imagine a ministry marked by power and self-control, but no love for the people (picture the pastor who is a well-oiled, efficient 'ministry-machine'). That kind of ministry will leave carnage in its wake. Have you seen that kind of ministry in action? Is that you, perhaps? Imagine a ministry marked by power and love, but no self-control. Such a pastor will burn out in a blaze of glory before too long. Have you seen it happen? Is that you? Imagine a ministry marked by love and self-control, but lacking power. It will be stuck in mud and lacking effectiveness. Have you seen that kind of ministry? Does it sound all too familiar and rather close to the bone?

In and of ourselves, you and I lack the power and love and self-control we need for Gospel ministry. But thank God for the gracious gift of his all-sufficient Spirit. Why not pray for the Father to fill your ministry afresh with the power, love and self-control of his Holy Spirit.

5

Are you ashamed or are you suffering?

So do not be ashamed to testify about our Lord, or
ashamed of me his prisoner. But join with me in
suffering for the gospel, by the power of God.... (1:8)

When we first started out as pastor-teachers, many of us will
have been wholehearted in our commitment to the gospel
and relatively unconcerned about what others thought of our
choice of work. After all, if we had been really concerned
about what others thought, we probably would have chosen
another, more respectable job. But as the years go by, some of
us find it more and more uncomfortable socially and, in some
cases, 'professionally', to hold to thoroughgoing evangelical
convictions. When our neighbours or other parents at the
school gate or unbelieving family members speak out in horror
about what they read in the papers on the intolerance of
Christians on gay marriage or another issue – we find it harder
and harder to do anything more than furrow our brow and stay
very quiet. If we are involved in large and mixed denominations
or, perhaps, academic institutions, we can find it increasingly
costly and limiting to stick with the apostolic gospel. Holding

to doctrines like penal substitution and the final authority of the Bible does not tend to increase our chances of becoming bishops or area superintendents or professors of theology. We discover more and more as time goes on that being unashamed of the gospel message and our fellow gospel ministers will cost us in all kinds of ways.

So Paul gives us a simple choice: Will we be ashamed of the gospel and of Paul (and, by extension, our fellow ministers now)? Or will we join with Paul and our faithful brothers and sisters in suffering for the gospel? Will we content ourselves with never progressing very far in our denominational or institutional hierarchy if that is what it takes? Will we be willing to be seen as outsiders (and worse) by the society around us? If it comes to it, will we be willing to proclaim that Jesus is the only way to God and that his Word is true, even if it lands us on the wrong side of the law of the land?

Paul takes it as a given that faithful gospel ministers will suffer. Indeed, all believers who seek to live godly lives should expect persecution (3:12). For Paul, his appointment as a 'preacher and apostle and teacher' is the reason 'why I am suffering as I am' (1:11-12). Even as he writes his letter to Timothy, he is enduring the physical discomfort and deep humiliation of prison for the sake of Christ. Paul's situation is so humiliating that he feels the need to urge his loyal friend Timothy not to be ashamed of him (1:8), mindful of the fact that many of his friends have simply abandoned him (1:15, 4:10). For Timothy, suffering is simply part of the job description: 'Endure hardship with us like a good soldier of Christ Jesus' (2:3; see also 4:5). Part of that suffering will come as he continues to stand by Paul in his humiliation, even while others move swiftly to distance themselves from the disgraced prisoner. We too will need to be prepared to suffer if we are resolved to stand by other ministers when they face scorn and rejection from within the church and from society at large.

I remember receiving the job description for my first paid ministry post as an assistant minister. The senior minister who was responsible for hiring me had put various things on the job description: he wanted someone who had theological training, who was a people person, who had a godly life, and so on. But as I read through the list one criterion leapt off the page: this pastor was looking for a ministry associate who was willing to suffer for the gospel. My first reaction was to wonder exactly what kind of congregation he was serving! But then I thought how shrewd it was to put that requirement on the person description for the job. For, if we are unwilling to share in suffering for the gospel (the gospel that proclaims a suffering Saviour, after all), we cannot be suitable for the job.

Suffering is never an attractive prospect and we would all naturally prefer to avoid it. In a sense Paul's call to suffer might seem entirely unrealistic, were it not matched with a reminder of the means by which we are to face suffering. We can only, and will only, join in suffering if we do so 'by the power of God'. God always gives us the resources to do what He has called us to do, and if we will obediently face suffering for the sake of his gospel, He will give us all the courage and resilience and faithfulness we need.

So, let me ask you: Are you suffering for the gospel by God's power, or are you ashamed of the gospel and its faithful ministers?

6

Are you heeding the holy calling?

> ...who has saved us and called us to a holy life—not
> because of anything we have done but because of
> his own purpose and grace. This grace was given us
> in Christ Jesus before the beginning of time.... (1:9)

The 'calling' Paul speaks of here is not a special 'calling' to ministry, but, as elsewhere in the New Testament, the general 'call' to live a holy life that accompanies salvation ('... who saved us and called us ...'). Paul wants to remind Timothy that he was saved from the consequences and power of sin in order to be set apart as 'holy' for the Lord Jesus. It is very striking that Paul takes the trouble in this letter to an experienced ministry colleague (who might be expected to know this already) to remind him that the Lord Jesus has saved him in order that he should live a holy life.

It is all too easy for us in positions of leadership in ministry to feel that we no longer need to be reminded of that basic expectation to live a holy life, and it is all too easy for others to assume that they no longer need to remind us. But Paul knows better than that; he knows that, although Timothy has been saved by the Lord Jesus and even set apart as a pastor-teacher, he is still a sinner and still has to do battle with a sinful nature – so he urgently needs to be reminded of the call to holiness.

The Ministry Medical

Timothy was in the privileged position of having the apostle Paul keeping an eye on him and reminding him of this basic truth. Perhaps the Christians in the local church at Ephesus would never have felt able to remind Timothy and might not have had the courage to challenge him if they sensed that his holiness was slipping. The elders at Ephesus certainly should have felt able to remind Timothy and should have been willing to do so. But if the believers at Ephesus might have hesitated to challenge and exhort Timothy to live a holy life, Paul certainly had no such reservations.

If you are in a position of Christian leadership and are well respected (even revered) where you are, I wonder if there are those around you who are challenging you on your personal holiness? Do you have the kind of people around you – perhaps, elders or close friends in the church, or others in Christian ministry – who have an open invitation to ask you hard questions about your holiness and challenge you where they feel you need to be challenged?

We all know stories of ministers who have lived a double life, preaching a message of holiness, but having somehow come to believe that the call to holiness no longer applied to them. Some of us will have seen at close range ministries implode spectacularly because of straightforward *unholiness* in the minister's life.

I am grateful to have a group of trusted and loyal Christian men with whom I meet every few months (and at least once a year) who ask me the hard questions, usually under the following alliterative headings to help us remember what to cover: *girls* (sexual purity; honouring marriage and treasuring our wives), *gold* (financial integrity and giving), *goals* (career and ambition), and *God* (our walk with the Lord Jesus; disciplines of Bible reading and prayer; and personal evangelism). We give each other permission to ask the tough questions, and then we pray for each other to keep going and to grow in holiness. I count those friends a gift from the Lord. If you don't have an accountability group like that, why not make a point of establishing one so that together you can help each other heed the calling to be holy?

7

Are you convinced that God will guard the gospel?

> Yet I am not ashamed, because I know whom
> I have believed, and *am convinced that he is able to*
> *guard what I have entrusted to him for that day.* (1:12)

Most of us in ministry go through seasons of feeling rather
pessimistic about the cause of the gospel in our local patch.
Growth often seems slow and opposition strong. Despair
easily sets in. Paul, in his particular situation, could easily have
given in to despair. Here he is, the great apostle, with bags of
experience and presumably a bit of fight left in him, locked
up in a Roman prison facing the prospect of death. He has
been abandoned by 'everyone in the province of Asia' (1:15),
deserted by a close ministry associate who was unwilling
to suffer alongside him (4:10), harmed greatly by those who
oppose him, and left with no one to speak in his defence at
his first trial (4:16). He knows that false teaching abounds and
false teachers prosper (2:16-18; 3:1-8) and that preachers of
the true gospel will receive no hearing in many quarters (4:3-4).
Nonetheless, he is fundamentally optimistic about the future;
he *knows* for certain that the true gospel will be preserved and
handed on until the final day.

The Ministry Medical

Some read 1:12 as saying that Paul is convinced that God will preserve what he (Paul) has entrusted to Him (God) until the day. But the trust or deposit is surely the gospel itself; Timothy is to hold to that 'pattern of the sound words' and 'guard the good deposit' that has been entrusted to him (1:13-14). Amidst all the discouragements and the storms of false teaching and the torrent of persecution against him, Paul is nonetheless entirely confident; God Himself will guard the gospel deposit that He has for a time placed in Paul's hands and in Timothy's hands too.

There is a particular lesson here for the older minister who worries that faithful ministry will not continue beyond his own generation. We are all prone to believe that we are rather more central to God's plans for the gospel than we actually are. As gospel ministers, we are privileged to be part of God's work and to have a role to play in his larger plans, but ultimately the preservation of the authentic gospel does not rest on any one pair of shoulders. God Himself is deeply committed to guarding the gospel and ensuring that it is passed on and proclaimed faithfully from one generation to the next. We must not imagine that once we put down the baton, the truth will cease to be proclaimed. Paul is confident, not simply because he knows Timothy to be faithful, but fundamentally because he knows that God Himself is guarding the gospel.

Whatever your situation and stage in ministry, are you rejoicing in the truth that God Himself is guarding the true gospel and has planned for its faithful stewardship and proclamation, right up until the Lord Jesus returns? In that sense, are you a gospel optimist?

8

Are you guarding the good deposit?

What you heard from me, *keep as the pattern of sound teaching*, with faith and love in Christ Jesus. *Guard the good deposit* that was entrusted to you—guard it with the help of the Holy Spirit who lives in us. (1:13-14)

Novelty in ministry is often very attractive, especially to younger ministers; but novelty needs to be handled with care. While it is helpful and necessary to think outside the box in terms of fresh and creative ways to communicate the gospel and to organise church, we must be those who avoid innovation at all costs when it comes to the message we proclaim. When it comes to our handling of the Word and our proclamation of the gospel, we are to take every step necessary to ensure that we neither add nor take away; we are simply stewards, guarding a deposit. Paul saw himself as a guardian of the gospel deposit, and he has passed on that deposit to Timothy. Timothy now possesses a fixed 'pattern of the sound words' and his job is to guard it with his life.

Timothy needed to be reminded that he was a steward and not an innovator because he was surrounded by those who modified the gospel to make it seem more attractive, and there was evidently a great hunger for distorted gospels around Ephesus. The latest fad was to believe that 'the resurrection has already taken place' (2:18), meaning that all the blessings of heaven and the new age are available now. It echoes very much the prosperity teachings so prevalent today in Africa, Asia and South America, and increasingly very much in evidence in the West as well. The call to suffer as a disciple of a crucified Lord and as a partner of an imprisoned apostle was a hard sell in Ephesus. But Timothy needed to be reminded to stay with the true gospel and guard it through believing it himself and proclaiming it to others.

We need the same reminder today. We need the reminder because there is still no shortage of false gospels, pseudo-gospels and skewed gospels on offer. We need the reminder because we will be instinctively fascinated with novelty. Theological movements such as the 'new perspective on Paul' and various updated versions of the social gospel have gained a hearing among mainstream evangelicals because they are new and interesting and sound fresh and exciting. But when we hear a message that sounds different from what we know to be the true gospel, our instinctive reaction should not be one of excitement and fascination, but of caution and sometimes alarm. We are stewards, not innovators.

Being a steward, of course, feels much less exciting and is much less prestigious than being an innovator. We won't steal headlines and attract the limelight by saying what has been said before. The danger is particularly great if we write books or are involved in academic work as part of our ministry, because so often the pressure in those spheres is precisely to find something new to say. But we must be those who are prepared to be decidedly unoriginal when it comes to the core of our message. Of course there is vitally-important creative work to be done in seeing how the 'unchanging Word' applies to our 'ever-changing world'.[1] But as we seek to be fresh and even

---

1.   Stott, *Preaching*, p. 144.

prophetic in our *application* of the word to our new day, we must be those who stick faithfully to believing and proclaiming the never-changing Word entrusted to us.

So we need to ask ourselves: in our own thinking and understanding and in our teaching and preaching, are we guarding the gospel deposit as humble stewards, or are we seeking the limelight as innovators?

9

Are you being strengthened by grace?

> You then, my son, *be strong in the grace that is in Christ Jesus....* (2:1)

In pastoral ministry we often feel as though we are jugs that are constantly being poured out – pouring out Bible talks and sermons, pouring out sympathy and concern, pouring out time with people, pouring out energy in administration, and the list goes on. Paul says of himself at the end of his ministry that he is 'being poured out like a drink offering' (4:6). But if we are those who are pouring out and being poured out, we must be those who are being filled up, enriched and strengthened. So, what is the source of our strength? Paul tells Timothy that he must 'be strong in the grace that is in Christ Jesus'.

In the New Testament 'grace' sums up all the riches we have in and through Jesus and his work for us. It has two closely-related aspects: God's redeeming grace and God's sustaining grace. In redeeming us from the penalty of our sin, God poured out his kindness toward us, giving his Son to bear our punishment in our place to make us righteous in his sight. It is God's redeeming grace in Christ that is particularly in view, for instance, when Paul says in Titus 2:11 that 'the grace of God that brings salvation has appeared to all men'. But God's grace to us in Jesus does not stop at the cross; the resurrection and the gift of the Holy Spirit shows us that his grace continues in sustaining us in the Christian life and making us more like his Son.

Here Paul tells Timothy to be sure that he is being strengthened in the grace that is in Christ Jesus. If Timothy is to keep going in faithful ministry (and not become a deserter like those mentioned in 1:15), he needs to be strengthened first by the redeeming grace of God. That is, Timothy needs to be resting on and rejoicing in the fact that God has graciously dealt with his sin and reconciled him to Himself. It is painful to be reminded of our sin and we often feel our failures particularly keenly when we are in positions of Christian leadership. We know that those who teach are held to a high standard of conduct and 'will be judged more strictly' (see James 3:1). When we do fail and when we are reminded of our sin (as we are so often), God in his kindness prompts us to remember his grace and to rejoice in what the Lord Jesus has done. Usually those weeks when we are most conscious of our own sin and our own need of grace we will preach more powerfully the truth of God's grace, for the good of our hearers.

We also need to be strengthened by the sustaining grace that is ours through our union with Jesus by his Holy Spirit; as Paul puts it so succinctly, through our being 'in Christ Jesus'. Paul has already reminded Timothy that his power to guard the gospel deposit is only 'by the Holy Spirit who lives in us' (1:14). Again, often God shows us our weakness and frailty in uncomfortable ways in order that we might lean all the more heavily on his grace. Mark Ruston, whose faithful ministry at the Round Church in Cambridge over many decades had such an impact for good, used to say of himself, 'I am weak as water'. So are we all. But there is all-sufficient, sustaining grace available to us through our union with Jesus. So, even if we feel very weak at the moment, we truly can 'be strong in the grace that is in Christ Jesus' as we rely on his power and not our own.

10

Are you entrusting the gospel to future leaders?

> And the things you have heard me say in the
> presence of many witnesses entrust to reliable men
> who will also be qualified to teach others. (2:2)

As we look at our diaries and the demands on our time, it will often feel like surviving through to next week and having something plausible to say on Sunday morning will take all the energy and resources we have. But Paul's vision looks well beyond next week, next month, next year, or even the next decade. He surveys the broad sweep of gospel ministry in the years to come and thinks of four generations at once, planning for what the church will look like in two or three decades' time. If that future church is to be marked by faithfulness to the gospel, Paul knows that Timothy needs to make some adjustments to his diary right now. Paul reminds Timothy that he has received the gospel trust from him. He has those two generations in his sights. But now he tells Timothy to pass on the gospel trust to others – not simply to those who will hear it for themselves, but to those who will be 'reliable' and 'qualified to teach others'. That's two more transfers, and two more generations. Paul is a strategist, with a long-term view.

The Ministry Medical

I wonder if you share Paul's horizon and his strategic vision for the future?

This work of entrusting the gospel to faithful men and women who will teach others involves a huge investment of time and a long-term commitment, not least because it is often done slowly and painstakingly, one-to-one. In his commentary on 2 Timothy, John Stott gives thanks to God for E.J.H. Nash ('Bash'), the man who led him to Christ and nurtured him in the early years of his Christian life: 'I thank God for the man who led me to Christ and for the extraordinary devotion with which he nurtured me in the early years of my Christian life. He wrote to me every week for, I think, seven years. He also prayed for me every day. I believe he still does. I can only begin to guess what I owe, under God, to such a faithful friend and pastor.'[1]

Bash was a strategist in the Pauline mould. He recognised that the future of gospel ministry required, in human terms, a focused investment in younger Christians with potential for godly leadership. He knew that it was no good sprinkling his efforts thinly on large numbers of young people; he saw that the most effective way to disciple future leaders and gospel ministers was to do 'a deep work in a few'. He invested time and prayer and Bible teaching in a few young men through his Scripture Union summer camp ministry. The result has been that a disproportionately large number of current leaders in English evangelicalism (particularly within Bash's denomination, the Church of England) have been nurtured through Bash and the ministry he established.

What is stopping you from investing your time and energy into future leaders? What prevents you from doing that deep work in a few, for the sake of the generations to come?

Let me suggest a few reasons why we may not invest in this way:

1. *Time is short.* We all feel busy. There are pressing demands on our time, and that means the important and strategic

---

1. Stott, *2 Timothy*, p. 29.

things often lose out to the immediately urgent things. But to fail to regard the work of passing on the gospel deposit to faithful future leaders as urgent and pressing is simply short-sighted. Perhaps we need to get our perspective right and recognise that this is more urgent than some of our hospital visiting or programme planning or fundraising. Perhaps this work of discipling future leaders needs to move up our priority list a few notches.

2. *We feel we have nothing to pass on.* We may feel inadequate for the task and too feeble in our own leadership to have anything useful to share. Perhaps we are nervous of allowing others to get too close to us and see how feeble we really are. We do of course need to be able to commend not only our message but also our lives to the younger people we disciple. So if our lives do not bear scrutiny, we should make a priority of addressing our own godliness. But the primary focus in discipling others is not on passing on ourselves, but on passing on the message. We are not to think of ourselves as life coaches, training up future leaders to be just like us; we are to see ourselves as Bible teachers, passing on the deposit that we ourselves have guarded. That is why we fulfil 2:2 not simply by befriending potential leaders of the future but specifically by investing time in opening up the Bible and training them from the Word. At the core of our strategy in training and discipleship must be considerable time set aside simply to teach the Bible to our potential leaders of the future.

3. *Our pride.* If we are not careful, our own pride will keep us from doing 2:2, and it will do so in a couple of ways. First of all we can convince ourselves that we are too important and our time too precious to invest one-to-one or with small groups of younger Christians who may or may not turn out to be leaders in the future. After all, we all know that investing in people is risky because some of the

people we pour our time and prayer into may turn out to disappoint us. Second, when we give ourselves to training up future Bible teachers, we will need at some stage to hand over Bible teaching opportunities to these young trainees. If I think that my church's ministry depends all on *me* and if I really love doing all the preaching and teaching myself, then I will not want to hand over opportunities, thinking it too much of a risk. But that is just our pride talking, and it is actually self-centred and short-sighted.

What are you doing to entrust the gospel to leaders of the next generation?[2]

---

2. In God's providence, on the day that I began drafting this chapter Trevor Archer (Director of Training for the Fellowship of Independent Evangelical Churches) was visiting the PT Cornhill Training Course to lead a session on ministry training in the local church. His reflections on 2 Timothy 2:2 and the discussion that followed were stimulating and helpful for my own thinking here.

11

Are you avoiding entanglements?

> Endure hardship with us like a good soldier of
> Christ Jesus. No-one serving as a soldier gets
> involved in civilian affairs—he wants to please
> his commanding officer. Similarly, if anyone
> competes as an athlete, he does not receive the
> victor's crown unless he competes according to the
> rules. The hardworking farmer should be the first
> to receive a share of the crops. Reflect on what
> I am saying, for the Lord will give you insight into
> all this. (2:3-7)

Paul has just reminded Timothy that he needs to prioritise the time-consuming work of discipling the next generation of gospel ministers (2:2). This is hard work and, as with all the work of ministry, will involve suffering (2:3). To help Timothy to get his priorities straight and give himself fully and self-sacrificially to the vital work before him, Paul sketches three images of single-minded devotion which are to be patterns for him and for us.

The first image is of a soldier. All gospel ministers are soldiers of Christ Jesus, their commanding officer. Good soldiers have as their undivided aim to please the officer over them. Only that kind of undivided loyalty will cut it in the thrust of battle where danger abounds and where the commanding officer needs to know that he can rely on his soldiers' full attention and complete loyalty. So Paul reminds us that no self-respecting soldier 'gets involved in civilian affairs' (or, as the ESV has it, 'gets entangled in civilian pursuits'). That is, he ensures that there is nothing going on in his life that will deflect and distract him from the urgent work before him. As his regiment passes through a town on the way to battle, he will see all the potential distractions and diversions of everyday life – most of them harmless enough in and of themselves – but he will not even contemplate stopping to pursue them. There is a divide between him and the civilian population which he must honour if he is to be effective as a soldier and so please his commanding officer.

If you are not a pastor-teacher, but are involved in some form of Bible-teaching ministry, the line of application of Paul's instruction here is not direct. It may be that you have a full-on career that is in many ways very '*entangling*', but you lead junior church on a Sunday morning or lead a home group Bible study during the week. You are not called to avoid every 'civilian' pursuit. But as a derived application, you should consider what it is you need to do to keep yourself free and unentangled for the particular ministry you have. Perhaps leaving the office promptly on a Wednesday night to be back in time for home group will cost you in terms of career advancement over the long run. Perhaps giving time on a Saturday morning to prepare your junior church lesson for the next day will mean that you have to give up playing sport at the weekend. Those may well be entanglements you need to avoid for the sake of your ministry.

However, for the full-time pastor-teacher (who is directly in view here), Paul's point is that there is a divide between you and the rest of the population which you need to maintain vigilantly if you are to be effective in your ministry and if you are to please the Lord Jesus. You need to be disciplined not to allow any entanglement – no matter how good or innocent it may be

– to undermine your ability to give yourself to the important work before you. This does not mean that the pastor-teacher is not free, for instance, to marry. After all Paul asserts his freedom to marry, but simply says that he has willingly chosen to forego that right (1 Cor. 9:5). It does not mean that you should not have other interests and hobbies. But it does mean that nothing must be allowed to entangle you, distract you, or slow you down.

Pastor-teachers who are married and perhaps have children need to handle this teaching carefully. It is all too easy for us to see our ministry to the wider church family as of primary importance and our commitments to our own immediate family as a distraction and even a burden (even if we would not put it quite so bluntly!). We may be really good at teaching the Bible to everyone else and unfailing in attending to the needs of everyone else – but culpably negligent in both when it comes to our spouse and children. We need to remember that we have a primary *ministry* responsibility to our own immediate family that is easily overlooked. As husbands and fathers (quite apart from our role as pastor-teachers) we are responsible for promoting the spiritual welfare of our wives and providing spiritual oversight for our children. Neglecting this primary responsibility is not only foolish and unkind, it actually disqualifies us from the office of elder (1 Tim. 3:5). As ministry-minded people, it may help us to get the balance right and invest the required time and interest in the spiritual welfare of our families if we remind ourselves regularly that God has given us a *ministry* mandate at home.

So we do not have here a mandate to ignore our families, nor do we have a licence to avoid all contact with the outside 'civilian' world and bury ourselves in our study under the banner of godliness (but really because that's where we prefer to be ….). Paul will later charge Timothy to 'do the work of an evangelist' (4:5), and that work is very hard to do if we never have any contact with the outsider. But we do have a clear instruction not to allow ourselves to be drawn away from our vital work by avoidable distractions.

Paul assumes that applying the principle of 2:4 to our lives will be costly; the instruction of verse 4 follows verse 3: 'Endure hardship with us like a good soldier of Christ Jesus.' One of the ways we share in suffering is by avoiding entanglements, and this *will* cost us: we will presumably miss out on economic opportunity, miss out on some recreation, and never develop some of our gifts and interests. You will notice, though, that Paul does not attach a detailed list of rules to this instruction. It is not as simple as 'Do not have a hobby' or 'Do not have any business interests' (Paul supported himself as a tentmaker after all). As so often is the case in the Bible, the instruction is left in general terms to be applied to our unique situation under the guidance of the Holy Spirit. Paul leaves it to us to consider the implications for ourselves: 'Reflect on what I am saying, for the Lord will give you insight into all this' (2:7).

12

Are you working hard?

> Endure hardship with us like a good soldier of
> Christ Jesus. No-one serving as a soldier gets
> involved in civilian affairs—he wants to please
> his commanding officer. Similarly, if anyone
> competes as an athlete, he does not receive the
> victor's crown unless he competes according to the
> rules. The hardworking farmer should be the first
> to receive a share of the crops. Reflect on what
> I am saying, for the Lord will give you insight into
> all this. (2:3-7)

The next two pictures Paul gives of single-minded devotion to the work of ministry are those of an athlete and a farmer. They both illustrate the sheer hard work involved in Word ministry. In order to maintain high standards at the ancient Olympic Games the rules stipulated that athletes had to have been engaged in intensive training for ten months prior to the competition.[1] Playing according to the rules meant arriving for

---

1.   Kelly, *Pastoral*, pp. 175-6.

the Games in a peak state of fitness.[2] It meant long hours at the gym before stepping on the track. Only those who put in the months of early mornings and hard sweats, of self-denial and strenuous training, could expect success when it came to the day. The related image of the farmer hardly requires comment. Only the farmer who sets his alarm early each morning, who toils in all seasons and all conditions, and who gives himself devotedly to the arduous task before him can expect to reap a crop and enjoy his share. Only the minister who gives himself fully to the work before him can expect, under God, to see gospel fruit from his labour.

When I took up my first full-time ministry post, I had come from a busy situation where I was in full-time secular work while carrying out part-time study alongside it. Although I knew better, I think there was just a little part of me that thought, 'Surely, this will be a bit easier than what I was doing before.' Little did I know! The following years would be full of joy in the privilege of ministry and of having time set aside for the Word, but they would add more lines to the forehead than my previous work ever did. Those who have never been pastor-teachers cannot understand the hard work involved. It is possible with little work to produce something to say on Sunday morning that is largely plagiarised from another preacher, or superficial and anecdotal, but involves no real engagement with what the Bible passage is saying. But really to grapple with Scripture and to understand what it meant in its original context and then to do the hard work of applying it both accurately and aptly to the contemporary world so that you and your congregation know what it means for us today – that takes very hard work. One

---

2. It is possible that the focus here is on adhering to rules governing fair participation rather than diligent preparation (see Mounce, *Pastoral*, p. 510). But given that the nature of the 'rules' is left unspecified here, we should look to the context of the surrounding metaphors to guide our interpretation. The context lends support to the idea that the 'rules' in view concern working hard, and so it seems best to assume that Paul does have in mind the rules that demand diligent preparation for the Games.

seasoned preacher suggested that a useful rule of thumb was to expect to spend one hour in the study for each minute spent in the pulpit. That may set the bar too high (especially if we have to prepare more than one sermon a week), but if we are inclined to leave sermon preparation until Saturday night, 2:3-7 calls us to a higher standard of diligence in sermon preparation.

Preaching takes hard work, and so too does the work of discipling individuals and families as an under-shepherd. People's lives are complicated and their spiritual needs often require a lot of time and care on the part of the pastor. Those of us who prize our time in sermon preparation may not go into ministry expecting to have to invest a lot of time in individuals, but that too is part of the work of the pastor-teacher. And we have not even begun to think about the practicalities of planning services and caring for a staff team and considering the administrative needs of sometimes large organisations.

The work of ministry is relentless and infinite. The pastor-teacher never goes to bed thinking: my sermon for next Sunday is flawless, the people under my care are now sinless, and my church programmes are humming along like finely-tuned machines. There is always more to do, and all of it takes time and hard work. More than that, we carry out the work knowing that we do so as those who will have to give account for the spiritual state of the souls under our care (Heb. 13:17). I never had that weight of responsibility in my previous secular employment – not even the C.E.O. of a multi-national company bears that level of responsibility!

There is, however, another side to this. While Word ministry properly understood and diligently done takes much hard work, it is also largely done unseen and is difficult to quantify. We can spend thirty-five hours on one sermon and five on another and most people in the congregation may not discern much difference. We can invest hundreds of hours in reading the Bible with a promising young person, and no one may know about it. Or we can never spend any time discipling anyone, and that failure may likewise go unnoticed. Many of the disciplines of ministry are private disciplines, and if we are given to laziness, we may get away with laziness for a long time. Our church or denomination may never call us to account for it. But, ultimately, the truth will out. So, let me ask you as I ask myself, are you working hard?

The two images that Paul gives us of hard work, that of the athlete and the farmer, have two goals set at the end of their horizon – a crown and a crop. These are not to be identified with the final salvation of the pastor-teacher. That is not what Paul is setting before the hard worker, or, by negative implication, threatening as loss for the lazy pastor-teacher. Victorious athletes received a wreath crown in the ancient Games and effective farmers enjoy a plentiful crop. Paul has elsewhere described the people to whom he has ministered as his 'crown' (Phil. 4:1; 1 Thess. 2:19) and the effect of gospel ministry in changed lives as 'fruit' (Col. 1:6). Paul has in view here the joyful prospect of a hard-working pastor-teacher seeing lives changed by the gospel as he labours in his ministry. If we're struggling to find the energy and motivation for our ministry at the moment, surely this joyful prospect is enough to prompt us afresh to work hard for the glory of the Saviour and the good of his people.

13

Are you thinking over what the Bible says?

> Reflect on what I am saying, for the Lord will give
> you insight into all this. (2:7)

It is interesting to reflect on the way the Bible works. We rightly insist that the Bible is clear and understandable; when God set out to make Himself known to us through his Word, He did so effectively. But to believe that the Bible is clear and understandable does not mean that it is always *easy* to understand (see 2 Pet. 3:16), nor does it mean that God gives us understanding the first time we read any given part of it. In fact, one of the characteristics of the Bible that convinces me that it is no ordinary book is its sheer depth of meaning. We can return to a familiar passage countless times and again and again find new meaning and new insight, new challenge and new help. In other words, God in his wisdom has given us a book that is perfectly understandable and effective, yet yields its treasure by degrees, not all at once.

This is part of the reason why preaching is hard work. It is not the case that we sit down with our English translation of the Bible on a Monday morning, read through the passage on which we will preach next Sunday, and know instantly what it means and how it applies to us and our congregation. It simply does not work like that. God could, of course, have given us a book that did function in that way. But in his wisdom He has given us the Bible we have. And He wants us to think it over. Since it is a verbal communication, this will mean looking carefully at the vocabulary God has moved the writer to use. (If we have or can acquire facility in Hebrew and Greek, that will be a great asset to us.) This will mean looking carefully at the way that words fit together into sentences and paragraphs and books. As with the study of all literature, it means giving careful thought to literary and historical contexts. We only know what individual words mean if we know how they were used both within the given Bible book in which they appear and in other literature of the time. Once we know what a sentence or paragraph or book is actually saying, we need then to think about how it applied to its first readers, and once we are clear on that, we then need to consider how it applies to us. We need to take into account the fact that although Bible books were not initially written *to us* they are nonetheless all written *for us* (see Rom. 15:4). The book of 2 Timothy is a prime example: it was written to Timothy but it is recorded in our Bible for us.

It is sobering to see that even Timothy, who was trained personally by Paul and to whom this letter was written, was warned that he would have to 'think over' what he was being told (2:7). How much more so will we. Paul does not tell Timothy here why his writing (and, by implication, the rest of Scripture) functions like this, but there is a clue: he tells Timothy in 2:7 that understanding will ultimately come from the Lord Himself. As we find that understanding the Bible is sometimes hard and takes time and effort, we are reminded that our abilities are finite and we are cast again on God for his help. The fact that the Bible functions as it does teaches us dependency, and that is especially true for the Bible teacher.

Many of us will find that the weeks where our preparation has been hardest – where we have had to wrestle with Scripture

Are you thinking over what the Bible says?

– are the very weeks when our preaching has been most effective. Sometimes in preaching preparation I find myself quite literally on my knees at my desk asking God for his help because I simply find that I cannot do it on my own. Here is not an invitation to 'let go and let God' when it comes to our study of the Bible. It is a call to hard work at the text in humble dependence on the God who gives understanding of his Word. This is at least part of the reason that the apostles insisted that they were set apart not only for the ministry of the Word but for '*prayer* and the ministry of the word' (Acts 6:4).

So we must be those who give time to thinking over what the Bible has to say and how it applies to us and the people under our care. We cannot hope to get those two related things right if we begin our sermon preparation on Saturday night. One seasoned preacher said to me recently that he likes to begin his preparation for a given sermon six weeks ahead of time. That much lead-time might be unrealistic for many of us, especially if we are in a situation where we are expected to preach two or more times a week on different passages. Nonetheless it is worth considering how we can begin our preparation early enough to spend time thinking about the passage and asking God for his help, both to get the meaning right and the application right. It may be that you are in a situation where you are simply not being given enough time to do this and your preaching is chronically thin because you have inadequate time for preparation. Perhaps it could be time for you to read through 2 Timothy with your elders or leadership team and even to reconsider your staffing situation and leadership structure.

Are you giving time, in prayerful dependence on the Lord, to thinking over what his Word says?

14

Are you remembering Jesus?

> Remember Jesus Christ, raised from the
> dead, descended from David. This is my gospel, for
> which I am suffering even to the point of being
> chained like a criminal. But God's word is not
> chained. (2:8-9)

I wonder if you have ever been in the situation where someone
(perhaps an older person) has taken you aside to tell you in an
authoritative tone something that you clearly already knew, and
it has all felt quite condescending and even a bit offensive. Just
imagine how Timothy may have felt as he opened his letter
from Paul and read chapter 2, verse 8. *Clearly*, Timothy had not
forgotten Jesus. *Clearly*, you and I remember Him too. But the
wise old apostle knew full well that Timothy needed to be told
to remember Jesus. So I take it that you and I need to be told
to remember Him too.

How, in the context of full-time gospel ministry, could we
possibly lose sight of Jesus Christ, risen from the dead, the
offspring of David, as preached in Paul's gospel? Proclaiming
Jesus and his message is our full-time job. There are at least two
ways that Timothy and we could fail to follow this instruction.

The Ministry Medical

The first is through *distraction*. It is easy to become so task-orientated and businesslike in our ministry – writing sermons, planning programmes, meeting with people – that we forget the Person who is the basis of our ministry, the subject of our proclamation, and the guarantee of our future hope. One of the ways we can check ourselves in this is to see how much we speak of Him generally and speak his name in particular. If all we ever talk about is 'the gospel' and 'serving the gospel' and 'trusting the gospel', but never speak of the Lord Jesus and serving Him and trusting Him – if our proclamation is always on the logic of the atonement in abstract terms but never on the work of Jesus in concrete historical terms – if *Jesus* is not at the centre of our thinking and believing and speaking and preaching, then we are forgetting Him, even as we get on with the business of ministry. I think we do this easily and frequently in evangelical circles, especially if we work in social contexts where allowing things (especially God-related things) to become too personal is rather difficult for both preacher and hearer.

The other and more serious way that we forget Jesus is through *distortion*. We all know that liberal theologians have distorted the Jesus of history in all kinds of ways over the last 150 years, and I presume that most of the readers of this book would not class themselves as theological liberals. So, surely this is not a danger for us. But Timothy was no liberal, and yet Paul felt the need to remind him which Jesus it was he needed to remember. Timothy was to remember the Jesus Christ of 'my gospel', 'raised from the dead, descended from David' (2:8). Timothy needed to remember the Jesus who is the Messiah, the royal offspring of David, God's promised King, who nonetheless died and then rose again. That is, Timothy needed to remember that this exalted royal Messiah nonetheless was the Messiah who suffered, died, and conquered death through his resurrection. This was always the Jesus Paul preached, the Jesus of the cross and resurrection. And it is for *this* Jesus of *this* gospel that Paul is suffering (v. 9).

Are you remembering Jesus?

Zooming out slightly to look at the context here will help us see why Paul is reminding Timothy of who the authentic Jesus is. He has urged Timothy to 'Endure hardship with us like a good soldier of Christ Jesus' (2:3) and then illustrated what that will involve. He will go on to speak of his own endurance of suffering for the sake of this Jesus and this gospel and then give Timothy a trustworthy saying to remember which speaks of the suffering that always precedes glory in God's economy (2:11-12). This talk of suffering in service of a suffering Messiah becomes all the more relevant when we come to see that in Ephesus there is a heresy doing the rounds that says that the resurrection of God's people has already happened (2:18). The word on the street is that real Christianity is a health-and-wealth, suffering free variety. If Timothy is to be willing to suffer, he will need to remember that Jesus was not only the King, but the King who suffered and died. And if you and I are going to embrace scorn (and possibly much worse) from outsiders and disdain from those even within our churches, along with all the other potential hardships of gospel ministry, we will need to remember that Jesus Himself died before He rose. Is the authentic Jesus at the centre of your ministry? Do you speak of Him and speak his name? Do you remember Him clearly enough to follow Him in suffering?

If we are not going to think ourselves above hardship, we will need to remember that David's royal offspring humbled Himself to the experience of death itself. If we are to have the courage to suffer, we will need to remember that for the true Jesus, death was not the final word; Paul's Jesus was 'raised from the dead' in triumph. And so too will we be raised.

15

Are you enduring for the sake of the elect?

> ...But God's word is not chained. Therefore I *endure*
> *everything for the sake of the elect*, that they too may
> obtain the salvation that is in Christ Jesus, with
> eternal glory. (2:9-10)

When ministry is hard and brings real suffering – on the low days when you can hardly remember why you took the job in the first place and you can hardly see how you can stick it out – what is it that keeps you going? What is it that keeps you from handing in your notice and finding something easier to do?

For Paul, who suffered more in his ministry than you and I are likely to in ours, the answer is simple: he endures all that he does for the sake of God's elect. Believing that the Word of God is unbound even though he himself is bound, and so being convinced that proclaiming the gospel will bear fruit, he presses on in his ministry for the sake of those whom God has chosen, both those who are already saved and those who will yet come to faith.

For Paul, the logic is simple. The proclamation of the gospel is a vital link in the chain of God's salvation plan. The conviction that preaching the gospel is vital in God's purposes underlies all of 2 Timothy and particularly the charge of 4:2 to 'preach the word'. Paul outlines his convictions in fuller detail in Romans chapter 10. There he reminds us of the great truth that 'Everyone who calls on the name of the Lord will be saved' (Rom. 10:13, citing Joel 2:32) and then asks a series of probing rhetorical questions: 'How, then, can they call on the one they have not believed in? And how can they believe in the one of whom they have not heard? And how can they hear without someone preaching to them?' (Rom. 10:14). The preaching of the gospel is God's chosen means of saving and then preserving his people.

This means that there is no more important work in the world than the preaching of the gospel. It is as simple as that. Paul wants the people to whom he ministers to 'obtain the salvation that is in Christ, with eternal glory' (2:10). That is, he wants them to be spared judgment and saved through the atoning work of Jesus, and he wants them, through their union with Jesus, to share in the eternal glory of his heavenly kingdom. Paul has judgment and eternity constantly in view. He is thinking of ultimate realities, and so as he faces persecution and shipwreck and imprisonment and, before long, execution, he is willing to endure it all and more for the sake of God's elect. He knows that the temporary cost attached to his ministry will fade into insignificance next to the eternal benefit enjoyed by the people he serves.

In enduring like this for the sake of God's people, Paul is not going beyond the call of duty. He is only doing in small measure what Jesus Himself did in an infinitely greater way. The salvation that is in Christ Jesus was only achieved as He gave Himself completely for us. For salvation to be achieved and for the message of salvation to be proclaimed, there must be suffering at every stage. 'You can't have a free Word without a bound apostle; you can't have a free gospel without a suffering Servant. The connection is absolute in this letter.'[1] As far as

---

1   Dick Lucas

suffering in gospel ministry is concerned, nothing has changed since Paul's day.

You and I will have to endure all kinds of things if we stick it out in gospel ministry for the long haul. It may well be that as you read this book you are yourself enduring painful trials in your ministry. What is it that keeps you going? There are plenty of gospel ministers who are enduring in unhappy situations for the sake of their pride ('it would be too humiliating to give up now') or their pension ('only seven years to go...') or for some other reason that is not the salvation of God's elect. If that is you, consider again the eternal realities and the central importance of your work as a gospel minister for the flock under your care and the yet unreached people of your community. And if you are barely enduring and are tempted to give up, adopt Paul's eternal perspective and ask whether your trials are worthwhile in light of the eternity stretching before the people to whom you minister. For Paul, all his suffering and enduring was made worthwhile 'that they too may obtain the salvation that is in Christ Jesus, with eternal glory'.

16

Are you reminding your people that there is suffering before glory?

> Here is a trustworthy saying: If we died with him, we will also live with him; if we endure, we will also reign with him. If we disown him, he will also disown us; if we are faithless, he will remain faithful, for he cannot disown himself. Keep reminding them of these things..... (2:11-14)

Paul is concerned that the Christians in Ephesus are in danger of forgetting some key truths, and he feels the need to prompt Timothy as their pastor-teacher to remind them. To put it simply, Timothy is to remind the Ephesian Christians that in the Christian life there is suffering now and glory later.[1]

First, suffering now. Jesus was very clear on the fact Himself: 'If anyone would come after me, he must deny himself and take up his cross and follow me. For whoever wants to save his life will lose it, but whoever loses his life for me and for the gospel will save it' (Mark 8:34-35). Timothy needed to remind the Ephesian Christians that following Jesus involves suffering. The latest pseudo-gospel doing the rounds at Ephesus conveniently

---

1.   I owe the summary of this section as 'suffering now, glory later' to my colleague Christopher Ash.

left out the suffering bit; it was all about the glory of the resurrection age now (2:18). Such a heresy would have had an easy appeal in a place like Ephesus, a major trade hub with lots of money and pleasurable distractions on offer. The Christians at Ephesus would have been entirely comfortable with the positive side of the promises Paul mentions: 'we will...live with him...we will reign with him'. But the call to die with Jesus (that is, to turn from sin and deny self) and then endure hardship with Jesus must have been very unpopular indeed. Paul knew that there would be a constant temptation for Timothy simply to leave those bits out of his proclamation in order to stop the haemorrhaging of his congregation to the false teachers, and so he prompts Timothy to 'remind them'.

All this sounds very contemporary. We who serve in the West operate in a context where standards of living have been rising more or less constantly since the Second World War and where disposable incomes have opened up a world of new pleasures to us. In such a context, it becomes harder and harder to hear and digest – let alone *proclaim* – a message that calls us to deny self and even to suffer. To our pampered Western ears, such a call is entirely alien. So, it falls to us pastor-teachers to make sure that we are taking the trouble to 'remind' our people of this call to die to self and to suffer for Jesus.

Dying to self means taking a radical and hard line with our sin. It means spending ourselves, not in our own service, but in the service of Jesus. It means not using our time and resources for self-indulgence, but instead making them available for the work of the gospel. It means enduring in following Jesus when the culture is turned against us and we find it hard going – even when outright persecution comes our way. Do the people in your church family know that this call to die and to endure suffering are part of the Bible's message, or have you been sanitizing it for them? We have just been working through the Christianity Explored Course in our home Bible study group; the final session of the course bears the rather unattractive but entirely appropriate title: 'Come and die'.[2] I wonder if that is the invitation you accepted when you turned to Jesus, and I wonder if it is the invitation you issue as a gospel preacher?

Next, future glory. Again, the Christians at Ephesus will have understood that being followers of Jesus was going to do them good, but some of them may have bought into the heresy that all the glory would be theirs in this life. So they urgently needed to see that the promises are for the future, resting on some big 'ifs' in the present ('*If* we died with him....*if* we endure....'). Timothy's job was to set the Christian hope before them as *future* hope. He needed to show the wonder and enormity of God's promises for the future and set those promises before his people so that they would be willing to deny self and endure in the present.

Again, I wonder if we are doing this faithfully in our own day? For many of us, life in the here and now is sufficiently pleasant that we are not inclined to think much about the hope of heaven. More than that, it all sounds a bit pie-in-the-sky to the sceptical ears of our contemporary culture. Rarely do I hear or give sermons on heaven or on our resurrection hope. Almost never do I hear or give a sermon dealing with the fact that 'we will reign with him'. But here it is in the Bible. If we really understood what the Bible teaches us about what it will mean to live and reign with Jesus in the resurrection age, we would find it much easier to live wholeheartedly and self-sacrificially for Him in the present age. And so would the people under our care.

Themes like glory of our future hope and the reality of dying to self and suffering in the present will be absent from our preaching if we have lost our cutting edge as ministers of the Word. When we ourselves lose our excitement about the gospel and our deep-rooted conviction of its truth and urgency, we will lapse into preaching a soft and easy discipleship that is focused on this present age. We will tell our people all that Jesus

---

2   *Christianity Explored Handbook*, 3rd ed. (Epsom, UK: The Good Book Company, 2011.)

can do for them in this life, but we will fail to lift their eyes to heaven and the glorious hope that we have, and we will refrain from calling our people to die and to endure.

So, let me ask you, are you reminding them of these things? If you recognise that you aren't, let me encourage you (as I encourage myself) simply to look afresh at Jesus as we encounter Him in Scripture – the Jesus who willingly died before He reigned, and who calls us to do the same.

17

Are you an unashamed workman?

> Do your best to present yourself to God as one
> approved, a workman who does not need to be
> ashamed and who correctly handles the word of
> truth. (2:15)

It is painful to see the fruit of incompetent workmanship. In October 2012 'Superstorm Sandy' ravaged New York City with flooding and powerful winds. One of the more striking photographs of the damage after Sandy passed through was of an apartment block with its front wall blown off in the storm. Although the building and its contents were otherwise intact, for two complete floors, the whole of the front wall was simply no longer there. From the road below observers could gaze into otherwise complete but utterly exposed living rooms and bedrooms of the apartments above. I have no means of verifying the cause, but I gather that shoddy workmanship has been blamed for the collapse. At some point, either in initial construction or in renovations conducted later, the integrity of the front wall was compromised, and the storm showed up its weakness in dramatic fashion.

The Ministry Medical

The fruit of shoddy workmanship eventually becomes plain to see, and the consequences can be catastrophic. As pastor-teachers we are workmen on God's precious building, his Church, and the quality of our work matters. The material we handle week by week is none other than God's own Word, the Word of truth.[1] Paul wants Timothy and us to receive approval for our work, to handle the Word correctly and to be unashamed on that final day when we stand before Jesus to give account for our ministry.

What does it mean to handle the Word correctly? It means, first of all, to understand it correctly in its original contexts, both historical and literary. It means finding out what was the situation (as far as we are told) of the writer and of the first readers of the book. Where were they in history and in the sweep of God's unfolding salvation plans? Why was this book written, to these people, at this time, and in this place? What was the big issue that the writer wanted to address? Before we know the answer to those questions (again, insofar as they are given in the Bible for any given book), we cannot begin to move toward application to our day.

Once we know the historical context of the book, we then need to look at the literary context of the particular passage we are preaching within that book. Why is the writer saying this here, at this point in his letter or book? What has come before in the previous verses and chapters, and what will come after? Often the answer to that question will give significant – even defining – shape to our understanding of the passage. Once we have that immediate context clear, we can get down to the hard work of grappling with the logic of the passage itself. What are

---

1. Kelly rightly points out, in light of Ephesians 1:13 and Colossians 1:5, that 'the word of truth' strictly refers to the gospel message (Kelly, *Pastoral*, 183). However, Paul is at pains to remind Timothy that the true gospel is 'my (*i.e.* Paul's) gospel', the apostolic gospel, (2:2, 2:8, 3:10), which is the same message proclaimed in all the Old Testament Scriptures (3:15). The Old Testament Scriptures and the Apostolic teaching of the New Testament record, define and proclaim the true gospel. So, for us, rightly handling the Word of truth means rightly handling God's written Word.

the main instructions? What are the logical links here? What does each word mean? Could I summarise the main thrust of the passage in a single sentence? At this stage I should have a pretty clear sense of the meaning of the passage in its original context, but there is still more work to do in handling the Word rightly.

Next, handling the word rightly must mean applying it accurately to our contemporary context. I am just about to start a sermon series on the book of Haggai. The big issue in Haggai is that the exiles have returned from Babylon and have been living back in Judah for some time, but the work on rebuilding the Temple has come to a standstill. Haggai has been sent by the Lord to rebuke his people for prioritising the building of their own houses while his house remains a ruin. How does that message apply to me and my church family today? The people originally addressed by Haggai lived thousands of years ago and quite a lot has happened since their day, not least the incarnation, death and resurrection of the Lord Jesus. There is no physical temple to be built today. So, even if I have a crystal clear understanding of what Haggai meant for its original hearers, I still have some hard work to do applying it accurately for today. To do that properly will require me to zoom out and think about the bigger sweep of God's salvation plan and where we stand in this present phase of that plan. There is no physical temple, but God's people – his Church – are his household. We are not given a physical building project, but we do have an urgent assignment to go and make disciples of all nations. And the fact of the matter is that we do tend to prioritise our own domestic concerns (the comfort of our homes, the security of our finances, the enjoyment of our holidays and hobbies) before the urgent assignment God has given us. So, there is a message for today. But it takes hard work and disciplined handling of the text to get there and to apply the Word accurately for today.

One of the ways we will know if we are not taking the care to handle the Word rightly is if all our sermons end up sounding similar and have more or less the same message. Some preachers have a knack for making any passage of the Bible teach their pet message, whatever that may be. But the Bible is rich and multi-faceted in what it has to say, and each passage and each book is there for a reason, because it offers something distinct. If all our sermons sound the same, we are preaching our message and not the Bible's, and so we are failing in our call to 'correctly handle the word of truth'.

Are you taking the time and care to understand the word rightly in its original contexts before jumping to a contemporary application? And having understood it properly, are you taking the care to apply it faithfully so that the applications you give to your people arise from the text and not from your own agenda or imagination?

18

Are you avoiding godless chatter?

Avoid godless chatter, because those who indulge
in it will become more and more ungodly. Their
teaching will spread like gangrene. Among them are
Hymenaeus and Philetus, who have wandered away
from the truth. They say that the resurrection has
already taken place, and they destroy the faith of
some. (2:16-18)

Paul has just reminded Timothy that he must do his very
best to present himself as an approved and unashamed
workman who handles the Word correctly. It seems that
Paul's particular concern here in the wider context is that
if Timothy does not discipline himself to handle the
Word rightly, he will become distracted and swerve away
from the big themes and clear teachings of the Bible into
debates about strange teachings that culminate in outright
distortions of the truth. Some Bible teachers at Ephesus
had done just that. Hymenaeus and Philetus evidently once

stood with the truth but have 'wandered away' or 'swerved' (ESV) from it in their teaching.[1]

Hymenaeus and Philetus provide a warning for Timothy and for us. At one stage they were doctrinally sound, holding to the truth. But they did not take care to 'correctly handle' the Word; or, more literally to 'divide' it or 'cut it straight', and so the result of their shoddy workmanship was that they 'wandered away from the truth'. It all may have started innocently enough. They got interested in debates about minutiae in Scripture and theological side issues. They enjoyed 'quarrelling about words' (see 2:14) to tickle their intellectual egos and they indulged in 'godless chatter', gaining a hearing and drawing attention by being a bit fresh and radical. You can imagine how the lie that the resurrection had already happened could have started out. Perhaps Hymenaeus and Philetus hosted a small group Bible study in one or other of their homes. They got talking one evening in their group about the word 'resurrection' and what it really meant. Someone in the group asked if it meant a physical raising or a spiritual one. Another person asked whether the gift of the Holy Spirit at Pentecost was not the start of the new resurrection life. And rather than squash the tangential discussion before it got out of control, Philetus and Hymenaeus enjoyed chairing it. And soon a rather attractive brand of false teaching was born, with two new hotshot theologians taking ownership of it and causing an attention-grabbing stir which they enjoyed. But what started out perhaps innocently enough leads to something much more sinister: their teaching spreads like 'gangrene', leading others into ungodliness (2:16-17) and upsetting the faith of genuine but undiscerning believers (2:18-19).

---

1. I say that they are Bible teachers; I assume that they held positions of authority in the church because they command a hearing and have sufficient influence to 'upset the faith of some'. Paul seems here to contrast Timothy the Bible teacher who is an 'approved workman' with these false teachers who most certainly are 'unapproved'. See Stott, *2 Timothy*, pp. 66-67.

Are you avoiding godless chatter?

Paul wants to make sure that Timothy avoids their error himself and guards the people under his care from following in it too. The only safe thing to do is for Timothy to 'avoid godless chatter' and to charge the people under his care not to 'quarrel about words' (2:14). Some debates and some discussions are not worth entering, even for the sake of correction. They should be avoided altogether. Theological debates that have nothing to do with the big themes and central concerns of the Bible – God's character and his glory, the ravages of sin and his plan of salvation, the future judgment and the Christian hope – such debates usually only take place to inflate the egos of the participants and can only cause harm.

Are you yourself keeping with the main line of the Bible and its big themes, or are you taking an unhealthy interest in minute theological debate and distractions? And are you encouraging your people to keep their eye on the main gospel themes of the Bible, warning 'them before God against quarrelling about words'? If you have been heading down side-tracks, perhaps Paul's instruction here is a timely prompt to set aside 'godless chatter' and to focus afresh on the glorious good news that lies at the very heart of the whole of God's Word.

19

Are you feeling youthful passions?

> Flee the evil desires of youth, and pursue
> righteousness, faith, love and peace, along with
> those who call on the Lord out of a pure heart.
> Don't have anything to do with foolish and stupid
> arguments, because you know they produce
> quarrels. And the Lord's servant must not quarrel;
> instead, he must be kind to everyone, able to teach,
> not resentful. Those who oppose him he must
> gently instruct.... (2:22-25)

The instruction of verse 22 is not saying what I thought it said
at first. I used to assume that the charge here was to avoid that
characteristic 'youthful passion' (ESV) of sexual lust. But in
Paul's mind, the characteristic passion of youth is not a lack
of sexual self-control but the inclination to be argumentative
and to pick fights. Rather than indulge this 'youthful passion',
Timothy is to pursue love and peace with all true and sincere
believers. Rather than indulge his love for a good argument, he
is not to 'have anything to do' with fruitless debates. After all,
'the Lord's servant must not quarrel', but instead be a kind and
patient teacher.

The Ministry Medical

We easily justify our argumentativeness. We are soldiers of Christ Jesus and defenders of the truth. Teachers who oppose the truth or distort the truth or simply fail to be clear on aspects of the truth need to be set straight – and who better to do it than me? And members of our churches who slow down gospel work or oppose our ministry or are just plain difficult to deal with – they are hindering the good gospel work that we are doing, and they need sorting out too, we tell ourselves. However, the difficulty is that we are called to gentleness and self-control. We are called to love the people under our care and to shepherd them, not bully them. We have all seen the disastrous fruit of ministers bullying members of their congregation. It is hugely damaging and brings dishonour to the Lord Jesus.

Similarly, we will have seen the fruit of ministries that focus on picking theological fights. There are some ministers and some churches who view themselves as the only remaining bastions of orthodoxy and who see it as their calling to identify and expose error wherever it may lurk. But a ministry set upon picking fights and dismantling opponents and their reputations runs contrary to what Paul instructs here. That is not to say that we should never expose error and teach against it. We should (see next chapter). But our ministries need to be characterised by the pursuit of 'righteousness, faith, love and peace, along with those who call on the Lord out of a pure heart.'

Are you fleeing the 'evil desire' to argue and are you instead pursuing peace? If you hesitate to answer that question, perhaps consider how your congregation might answer it? Or the other ministers in your denomination? Paul recognises that for the young man Timothy (as for many of us), fighting may come more naturally than peacemaking, and so he urges him to 'flee' his passions and 'pursue' the characteristics of a peace-loving ministry. May God give each of us the grace to do the same.

20

Are you correcting opponents with gentleness?

> Flee the evil desires of youth, and pursue
> righteousness, faith, love and peace, along with
> those who call on the Lord out of a pure heart.
> Don't have anything to do with foolish and stupid
> arguments, because you know they produce
> quarrels. And the Lord's servant must not quarrel;
> instead, he must be kind to everyone, able to teach,
> not resentful. Those who oppose him he must
> gently instruct, in the hope that God will grant
> them repentance leading them to a knowledge of
> the truth, and that they will come to their senses
> and escape from the trap of the devil, who has
> taken them captive to do his will. (2:22-26)

Dealing with theological opposition and false teaching with
faithfulness and godliness is one of the more significant
challenges facing the pastor-teacher, especially if we serve in
a theologically mixed denomination.[1] It is helpful to see here

---

1. I owe much here to Peter Adam and his perceptive treatment of this section of
   the letter. Especially helpful is his suggestion, which I follow, that Paul outlines
   two strategies for dealing with two different kinds of opponent.

that Paul expects that within the visible church in this age there will always be a mixture of converted and unconverted, faithful and unfaithful teachers of the Word. We have already thought about Hymenaeus and Philetus and their heresy in 2:17-18. We will go on in 3:1-9 to consider the impostors who follow in the footsteps of the men who opposed Moses long ago. In 2:20 Paul warns Timothy that in a 'large house' such as the Church of God 'there are articles not only of gold and silver, but also of wood and clay; some are for noble purposes and some for ignoble.' That is, the visible Church is a mixed place, and some teachers ('vessels' at least includes 'teachers' here, even if it includes non-teachers as well) will be dishonourable. This is not to say that we should content ourselves with a church structure that has no discernment in its appointment of leaders and no disciplinary structure for the removal of unfaithful teachers (we must have a robust structure that does both), but it is to say that we should not be shocked when false teachers come along and when other leaders oppose us when we faithfully teach the truth.

Here in this section of his letter (really from 2:14 to 3:9) Paul outlines two different strategies for dealing with two different kinds of opponents. There are, on the one hand, opponents who 'call on the Lord out of a pure heart' (v. 22) and who may be correctable (v. 26). On the other hand, there are corrupt impostors who look like Christians and seek to exercise influence, but are actually not converted (3:5, 8); they are to be avoided (3:5) and we should not waste our time with them.

In 2:22-26 Paul deals with the first kind of opponent: misguided people who are true believers, calling on the Lord out of a pure heart, and who need gentle correction, not excommunication. Paul recognises that Timothy's natural inclination will be to argue with opponents like this, but he is to flee that youthful passion and instead pursue 'righteousness, love, and peace' with other true believers, even if they are wrong in what they are teaching. His aim must be to convince them of the truth through gentle instruction from the Word in the prayerful hope that they will be given the gift of repentance and escape the devil's trap. In other words, his concern must be not to win the argument but to win the person.[2]

In practice this may mean spending more time engaging with other ministers within your denomination who you feel are misguided theologically. It may mean investing the time in attending ministry fraternals, or taking the initiative to set up a fellowship group or reading group with other ministers in your area. It may mean offering to read the Bible one-to-one with members of your church who are in particular need of instruction and doctrinal correction.

Who in your church or your denomination is misguided and opposing you, but nonetheless a true brother or sister in Christ who calls 'on the Lord out of a pure heart'? What has been your approach to them so far? Motivated by the prayerful hope that God might 'grant them repentance', what steps could you take to instruct them gently in the truth?

---

2   Peter Adam.

21

Are you avoiding 'such people'?

> But mark this: There will be terrible times in the last days. People will be lovers of themselves, lovers of money, boastful, proud, abusive, disobedient to their parents, ungrateful, unholy, without love, unforgiving, slanderous, without self-control, brutal, not lovers of the good, treacherous, rash, conceited, lovers of pleasure rather than lovers of God— having a form of godliness but denying its power. *Have nothing to do with them.* (3:1-5)

There are certain kinds of false teachers and opponents in whom we should not invest energy and time, but whom we must take care to avoid. Such people are not true followers of Jesus. Their love is not for God or for all that is good, but instead for self, money and pleasure. Their minds are corrupted and they are disqualified as far as the faith is concerned. So far, so obvious. The problem with these kinds of false teachers is that they have a 'form' or 'appearance' (ESV) of godliness. There is a certain superficial plausibility about them. They are not wearing a sandwich board with the word 'charlatan' emblazoned on it. Instead, they are pastors of churches and local evangelists. They are writers of Christian books and TV preachers. They are lecturers at theological colleges and presiding bishops. Paul tells us that such people 'worm their way into homes and gain control over weak-willed women....' (v. 6). That is, they exercise leadership and wield influence. People listen to them and are taken in by them. Paul wants Timothy and us to be prepared for such people to appear at regular intervals; their existence is a characteristic of our final age of salvation history (3:1)

There is only one approach to take with such people: have nothing to do with them. Back at the end of chapter 2 Paul has described the church as a great house filled with different kinds of teachers who are depicted as 'vessels' (ESV)—some wood and clay vessels used for cleaning and removing waste, some gold and silver vessels used for formal meals. Paul, of course, wants Timothy to be and remain a vessel set apart for 'noble purposes', and the only way to do that is to make sure that there is a clear distinction for all to see between him and the other teachers: 'If a man cleanses himself from the latter, he will be an instrument for noble purposes, made holy, useful to the Master and prepared to do any good work' (2:21). Being a useful and noble 'vessel' (read 'pastor-teacher') means putting clear blue water between you and unconverted, ungodly, truth-denying false teachers.

This is a message that will apply most pointedly to those who serve within mixed denominations where there are clearly ungodly, truth-denying unbelievers in positions of every level of leadership. It will take great courage for you to do that if that is your situation. But pastor-teachers who preach the truth yet pretend that unfaithful ministers in their denomination are sound and reliable compromise themselves and put their people at risk. There is only one safe approach to take when it comes to ungodly, truth-denying false teachers: 'Have nothing to do with them.' (3:5) That will be costly, but notice as well the great benefit: if we seek to be faithful in this way, we can hope to be instruments set apart 'for noble purposes, made holy, useful to the Master and prepared to do any good work' (2:21).

22

Are you continuing in what you have learned and believed?

> ...while evil men and impostors will go from bad
> to worse, deceiving and being deceived. But as for
> you, *continue in what you have learned and have become*
> *convinced of*, because you know those from whom
> you learned it, and how from infancy you have
> known the holy Scriptures, which are able to make
> you wise for salvation through faith in Christ Jesus.
> (3:13-15)

The false teachers at Ephesus evidently had the reputation of being rather *avant-garde* and innovative. They were the go-ahead, progressive types. In all probability they described themselves in these terms. But three times in this letter Paul speaks of their 'progression', not as positive innovation, advancement, and improvement (as the false teachers would have seen it), but with deep and sad irony, as progress away from the truth and from salvation itself. The 'godless chatter' of Hymenaeus, Philetus and their kind will not lead their hearers to salvation, but 'it will lead ['advance'] people to more and more ungodliness' (2:16, ESV). The false teachers described in 3:1-9, whatever they may think of themselves, 'will not get ['advance'] very far because, as in the case of those men, their folly will be clear to everyone' (3:9). Here in 3:13, 'evil men and impostors will go ['advance'] from bad to worse, deceiving and being deceived'. Heresy usually starts out under the banner of progress and innovation. It is usually lauded as advancement. The whole liberal movement of the nineteenth and twentieth centuries (which led to much heresy) began by looking beguilingly innovative. Soberingly, much of the impetus for liberal theology came from a desire to spread the gospel by making it more palatable to modern society.

Against this backdrop of 'advancement' and innovation – so-called 'progress' – Timothy is to make it his business to 'continue' with the true gospel that he has been taught. He is to resist the urge for finding a new interpretive edge on the Bible. He is to resist the temptation to modify the gospel to make it seem more attractive. He is to be very careful to avoid the trap of believing that his forebears were quaint and narrow-minded and that the message he once learned must now be updated for a new day. Timothy knows the integrity of his teachers – Paul, his mother and grandmother (1:5) – and the integrity of the Scriptures, and so he is to stick with the reliable and true message he received. It is very striking that more than once we are commended in the Bible to look back to the character and reliability of our former teachers to keep us from losing our balance theologically. Paul is doing that here. The writer of Hebrews does the same thing: 'Remember your leaders, who spoke the word of God to you. Consider the outcome of their way of life and imitate their faith' (Heb. 13:7).

When I was a student reading theology I remember coming across liberal theology really for the first time at the age of 19. It was both intellectually and spiritually disturbing, and I did not have the means to sort out all the issues there and then. But I remember reading 2 Timothy 3:14 at a particularly low point and going back to basics. I looked back to some of the people who had taught me the gospel in the early years of my

Christian life and considered their character and godliness, and remembered again the ring of truth and authenticity that surrounded what they said to me. The fruit of the gospel in their lives attested to the truth of their message to me. I then considered the character of some of the people who were calling into question the authenticity of God's Word, and it seemed to me that they lacked the marks of authentic godliness (although I thank God for the many godly teachers I did have at that time). And so, before I could come up with a good intellectual response to the new and distorted teaching I heard, the character of my respective teachers decided it for me.

Think back to the people who taught you the gospel and discipled you in ministry. Have you moved away from the doctrine they taught you, feeling that you have grown up a bit and become rather more savvy, or are you continuing in what you have been taught? It may be, of course, that you were evangelised and discipled by well-meaning people who had some shaky theology, and so it has been right to question some things they taught you. But if they were godly people who taught you faithfully from God's Word, it is worth asking whether you have 'moved on'. If so, be cautious. Of course the final standard is Paul's apostolic teaching in the Bible, and ultimately what we need is simply to stay with biblical doctrine. But it is possible to think that we are discovering new biblical angles which our forebears were not clever enough to see, but which, when scrutinised in the clear light of day, are actually pure distortion.

Are you *going ahead*, or are you *continuing on* in what you have been taught?

23

Are you using Scripture?

> the holy Scriptures, which are able to make you
> wise for salvation through faith in Christ Jesus.
> All Scripture is God-breathed and is useful for
> teaching, rebuking, correcting and training in
> righteousness, so that the man of God may
> be thoroughly equipped for every good work.
> (3:15-17)

Normally when I hear these verses taught it is in the context of establishing the authority of Scripture. They certainly do establish the authority of Scripture in their affirmation that it is 'breathed out by God'. But the primary emphasis here does not fall on the authority of Scripture; it falls, rather, on its sufficiency. Paul wants Timothy and us to see that Scripture is not merely the authoritative basis of our ministry, but the completely adequate tool for every task we undertake in ministry.

I take it that most people reading this book would adhere to a theologically high view of the reliability and authority of Scripture. The challenge for us is not so much believing that Scripture is true, but rather trusting that it is all we need. Peter

The Ministry Medical

Adam shrewdly comments that the question he would like to be able to ask in 20 years of his students from theological college is not, 'Do you believe the Bible?', but 'Are you using the Bible?'. It is easy for us to sign up to an evangelical doctrine of Scripture and to hold to it formally throughout our ministry, but simply to move on to other things as time goes on because we find that the church is not growing as we would like it to, or because we are getting weary of working hard at the text in our preaching, or because our congregation is getting tired of Bible teaching and hungry for something fresh and different. So we drift away from preaching the Bible and from using it in every area of church life.

If you see that happening in your ministry, you need to realise again what Scripture can do. The 'sacred writings' (and the Old Testament is in view here in the first instance) 'are able to make you wise for salvation through faith in Christ Jesus'. Do you believe that? Do you believe that the whole Bible – not only the New Testament, but the Old as well – is fully sufficient to bring people to salvation through faith in Jesus? Or, to put it in more practical terms, do you use the Bible in your evangelism? If you do not and would not, it must be because you do not believe that the Bible is God's mighty Word that can, in the power of the Spirit, bring life to the dead. Remember, after all, how you were brought to faith. You and I and every other believer 'have been born again, not of perishable seed but of imperishable, through the living and enduring word of God' (1 Pet. 1:23). God saves people through the power of his Word. If your evangelism bypasses the Bible, then you must lack confidence in the Bible. Whatever your theoretical doctrine of Scripture, if you are not using it, it *must* be the case that you do not trust it. More than that, if your evangelism bypasses Scripture, you should not expect people to come to new life through your efforts.

Notice what else the Bible is good for: 'teaching', 'reproof', 'correction', and 'training in righteousness'. That is, whatever pastoral or theological issue we face in our church, the Bible is sufficient to deal with it. Whether we are in the pulpit preaching on a Sunday morning, or visiting a dying person in hospital, or confronting a church member in the grips of a sinful lifestyle, or training a younger person for ministry – whatever we are doing and need to do, the Bible is completely sufficient. That does not mean that we refuse to buy or use any other book or resource; of course there will be a whole range of Bible-based resources that inform and help our ministry. But if the Bible is not at the heart of all our teaching and preaching, our pastoring and mentoring, we are not doing ministry God's way, and we are proving that we lack confidence in the powerful sufficiency of God's Word. The Bible has been given to us that 'the man of God' (probably meaning 'the spokesman of God'; here, the pastor-teacher)[1] 'may be thoroughly equipped for every good work'. Do you ever, like me, feel ill-equipped and under-equipped for your ministry? Well, let's get out our Bibles and trust God with the results.

Our practical doctrine of Scripture will be seen in our use of Scripture in every area of ministry. Are you using it?

---

1. In the Old Testament the term was used to refer to God's prophets and spokesmen; see Deuteronomy 33:1 and Psalm 90:1 (of Moses), 1 Samuel 9:6 (of Samuel), 1 Kings 17:18 (of Elijah) and 2 Chronicles 8:14 (of David).

24

Are you preaching in light of the end?

> In the presence of God and of Christ Jesus, who
> will judge the living and the dead, and in view of
> his appearing and his kingdom, I give you this
> charge: Preach the Word.... (4:1-2)

Our ministry will only stay on track if we really believe that Jesus is coming back to judge the world. If we do not believe that and if we fail to keep the coming judgment firmly in view all the time, we will certainly lose our way.

Paul is building up to the climax of 2 Timothy which comes in 4:2. The charge to 'preach the word' is at the very heart of this letter and of Paul's concern for Timothy. But the context in which this charge is given is definitive. Paul issues the charge and expects Timothy to follow it in light of the fact that Jesus will return to judge. Why is the prospect of judgment so central to Timothy's preaching ministry and ours? There are two reasons for its central importance.

The first is that our hearers will face the judgment. The simple and uncompromising truth is that Jesus will return and will send to hell those who have not turned from sin and put their trust in Him. He has appointed the preachers of the gospel to be his early warning system for the world and the means by which salvation is made available. We have a message that can provide safety when the day of disaster comes. We have a message that offers life to the dying. Remember how Paul summarises the Christian hope near the start of the letter when he writes of God's 'purpose and grace …. given us in Christ Jesus before the beginning of time, but … now … revealed through the appearing of our Saviour, Christ Jesus, who has destroyed death and has brought life and immortality to light through the gospel' (1:9-10). Ours is an urgent message. The people sitting under our ministry and those in our local area desperately need to hear it if they are to enjoy life and escape death. And so we must preach the gospel in light of the coming day for the sake of our hearers.

The other aspect of this is the fact that we ourselves are accountable to Jesus the Judge for our faithfulness in our ministry. I have already mentioned Hebrews 13:7 and the fact that we leaders will give account to the Lord Jesus for the souls under our care. It must mean great loss for us if we appear before Jesus and He asks us why the souls under our care did not know and understand the gospel or why they remained immature and unproductive in their faith. That thought must sober us and focus our preaching. Remember again Paul's words to the Ephesian elders in Acts 20: 'Therefore, I declare to you today that I am innocent of the blood of all men. For I have not hesitated to proclaim to you the whole will of God' (Acts 20:26-27). Will you and I be able to say the same at the close of our ministries?

25

Are you preaching the word?

> In the presence of God and of Christ Jesus, who
> will judge the living and the dead, and in view of
> his appearing and his kingdom, I give you this
> charge: Preach the Word.... (4:1-2)

The word Paul uses here to issue this central charge to Timothy
– the word 'preach' (*kerysso*) – means to 'declare' or 'proclaim
aloud', and it implies that there is an authoritative and urgent
message to proclaim. It defines this basic activity of Timothy's
ministry and ours in three key ways.

First, it shapes the way we *speak* about preaching. Along
with the very welcome resurgence of expository Bible ministry
here in the UK in recent years has come the habit of referring
to preaching regularly (and almost by default) as 'teaching the
Bible'. This, of course, is accurate on one level. Preaching at
its very heart is teaching. But preaching is not merely teaching;
it is much more than that, and habitually describing preaching
as 'teaching the passage' reduces the scope and gravity of the
exercise. As Paul goes on in verse 2 to tell Timothy what will
be involved in preaching, 'teaching' is there on the list, but it is
not the sum total.

The Ministry Medical

Second, the charge to 'preach' the Word defines the *style and demeanour* of what Timothy and we are to do. Preaching is a declarative act. It is not simply that Timothy is to point out a number of things from the Word and leave his congregation to think about it and come up with the answers and applications themselves, as though he were leading a small group Bible study. It is not as though he were making suggestions from the Word about what his people might like to believe and how they might choose to behave. He is to declare the truth of God's word. While he may lack confidence in himself, Timothy's authority comes from God's own Word which He has 'breathed' (3:16). The Scriptures themselves are Timothy's authority and equipment for this work of declaration (3:17). Timothy is to preach as one who reverently expects the return of Christ and so sees the urgency of his task (4:1). He is to assume the obligation to do so recognising that God Himself has given the leaders of his church the right and duty to set apart preachers ('In the presence of God and of Christ Jesus…I give you this charge…', v. 1). Timothy has been set apart for preaching by the apostle and the church elders (see 1 Timothy 4:14); and so preach he must. Preaching is a declarative act, carried out with all boldness, on the front foot, and not in timidity.

How about your preaching? Could it be described as declarative? Is it an announcement of the truth of the Word? Or is it marked by timidity and reserve?

Third, the fact that Timothy's task is to 'preach' shapes the *content* of his sermons. Had Timothy been set apart merely to 'teach the Bible' his sermons would be explanations of the logic of a passage of the Bible, perhaps with a bit of history thrown in, and maybe with a nod to application tacked on the end for good measure. But Timothy's job is to proclaim and declare God's Word, and so he is to 'correct, rebuke and encourage—with great patience and careful instruction.' (4:2). It is not simply that he lays out for his people the logic of a book or passage and then stops there. He certainly does that (part of the job is 'teaching'). But he is to move beyond understanding the Word to the impact of the Word on heart and life. He is to 'correct' his people when the Word shows up the fact that their thinking is wrong. He is to 'rebuke' his people when the Word shows up that their living is ungodly. He is to 'encourage' (including the stronger sense, 'exhort', ESV) his people to change in light of what they see in the Word and to live it out. Were he simply 'teaching the Bible' he would not feel able to go that far; but since he is 'proclaiming' the Word, he must go all the way.

The Bible does not contain very many examples of preaching for us to observe, but it does contain a few. Consider Peter's sermon at Pentecost in Acts chapter 2. He opens up the prophet Joel and shows the people before him that the last days have arrived, as demonstrated by the gift of the Holy Spirit. He does not then say to the people of Judah, 'You might like to go home and consider how this applies to you....' No, he rebukes them: 'Men of Israel, listen to this: Jesus of Nazareth was a man accredited by God to you by miracles, wonders and signs, which God did among you through him, as you yourselves know. This man was handed over to you by God's set purpose and foreknowledge; and you, with the help of wicked men, put him to death by nailing him to the cross' (Acts 2:22-23). If that were not clear enough, Peter drives in the knife even further: 'Therefore let all Israel be assured of this: God has made this Jesus, whom you crucified, both Lord and Christ' (Acts 2:36). And, not surprisingly, there was a response to that declaration of the truth: 'When the people heard this, they were cut to the heart and said to Peter and the other apostles, "Brothers, what shall we do?"' (Acts 2:37). And the result was that 'about three thousand were added to their number that day' (Acts 2:41). Peter did not get up and simply 'teach the Bible' at Pentecost; he got up and declared the Word with all boldness and authority, and the people were cut to the heart and thousands of lives were transformed for eternity.

The Ministry Medical

Does your preaching move from teaching to declaration; to reproval, rebuke and exhortation? Is there some challenge to respond to when your congregation goes home, or are they only left with truths to think about and to discuss politely over lunch? Have you lost your declarative edge? If you sense that you may have lost that declarative edge, let me encourage you to delight afresh in the powerful tool that God has given us in his authoritative life-giving Word. Our confidence to declare the truth with boldness never rests in ourselves, but in the God who graciously speaks through his Word.

26

Are you preaching in season and out of season?

> Preach the word; be prepared in season and out of
> season.... (4:2)

My grandfather tells a story of his experience as minister of
a church in Johannesburg in the 1960's. He arrived at this church,
which had the name of being evangelical, to find that many
in the congregation and leadership team simply did not know
the gospel. Soon after he began his ministry there, he attended
a national conference for pastors on the subject of spiritual
revival. In the course of the conference, his predecessor as
senior minister addressed the younger minsters in attendance.
With tears in his eyes, this older minister confessed to the
crowd that he had been culpably unfaithful in his ministry and
pleaded with them not to do what he had done. He went on
to say that he had arrived as a younger man to lead this smart
middle class church and found that the gospel received a frosty
reception among some of the well-heeled and sophisticated
members of the congregation. And so he decided not to preach
it. He confessed that for the twenty years he had been in that
post, he had not preached the gospel. He knew the gospel and
said he believed it; he had preached it in other churches, but he

refrained from preaching it in this one. The result was a church in which many thought they were Christians, but in reality had no idea what the gospel message was.

Paul sees that Timothy is heading for an era when the gospel will receive a frosty reception among the worldly and prosperous residents of Ephesus, and so he charges him to be ready to preach the Word 'in season and out of season'. This phrase, 'in season and out of season' could refer to Timothy's own preparedness and convenience to preach the Word, that of his congregation to receive it, or that of his surrounding culture to hear it. It seems to me that all three are potentially in view.[1] That is, he is to preach the Word faithfully whether it seems like just the right time or not, whether it is convenient or not, whether it will be well received or not. He is to preach it all the time, without prejudice or favour, and without fail.

There will be seasons in our own lives as ministers when we find preaching the gospel harder than at others. Our own hearts may be feeling cool and we may be going through a bit of a dry patch spiritually. We must not be so self-indulgent as to starve the people in front of us because we do not really feel like proclaiming the Word. The people before us will face the judgment, and they need to be ready (4:1). And we will have to give an account of our ministry on that day as well. We are to be always ready, preaching the true gospel whether we feel like it or not.

There will almost certainly be times in our ministry when some people in our churches will be less receptive to the Word and even quite hostile to elements of it. Timothy was to anticipate such seasons: 'For the time will come when men will not put up with sound doctrine. Instead, to suit their own desires, they will gather around them a great number of teachers to say what their itching ears want to hear. They will turn their ears away from the truth and turn aside to myths' (4:3-4). We will face battles over the truth with true believers in

---

1. Similarly, Green, *Finishing*, pp. 137-8.

our own church family. Such a time is no time to fall silent. Like that minister in South Africa, we will find that there are people within our churches who are not converted and so oppose the gospel. We will never do them any spiritual good by watering down the truth, imagining that a time will come further on down the track when the unconverted will grow to like the gospel more. We will only serve them usefully and discharge our ministry faithfully if we simply press on with preaching the Word.

There will be frequent seasons – in fact, this is probably the norm – when the world around us will not only be uninterested in what the Bible says, but will be downright hostile toward it. In that sense, our preaching will normally be 'out of season'. But we press on anyway, willing to endure the hostility that comes, and trusting God with the result. It is no wonder that Paul will again remind Timothy to 'endure suffering' (4:5).

What season are you in? What season is your church in? Are you preaching the Word faithfully and in its fullness, whatever the season?

27

Are you reproving, rebuking and exhorting?

> Preach the Word; be prepared in season and out of
> season; correct, rebuke and encourage—with great
> patience and careful instruction. (4:2)

We are all wired differently. Some of us will be more inclined to play good cop in the pulpit and some of us naturally will be more inclined to play bad cop. What I mean is that some of us will instinctively lean more toward comfort, gentleness, and reminders of grace in our preaching, while others of us will be more inclined to point out our people's sin and failings and to warn them of judgment. Neither of those extremes represents a biblical balance, and so it is important for us to know which way we naturally lean so that we can discipline ourselves to stay in tune with God's Word.

Here in 4:2, Paul is warning Timothy against going too easy on his congregation and he is calling him to say some of the hard things that need saying. Timothy needs to reprove his people when their understanding of God's Word is wrong. He needs to be willing to call error 'error' and then to correct it. He needs to rebuke his people when he sees that they are being ungodly in their behaviour. This will usually involve private rebuke where the sin is personal and private, and public rebuke when the sin is corporate and in the open. He needs to drive the applications of his preaching home by 'encouraging' (or 'exhorting') his people with appropriate challenge and urgency to live in light of what the Word says and to make the changes to their thinking and living that it demands.[1]

It is possible to have a ministry that is almost exclusively positive in tone. Such a ministry will rarely mention judgment, but it will always (quite rightly) mention grace; it will rarely make uncomfortable demands of people, and going to church under such a ministry will generally feel like having a good soak in a warm bubble bath. Such a ministry will have no cutting edge because error is not corrected and sin is not really dealt with. It may well fill a church with ready hearers and it will almost certainly be exercised under a banner of evangelical orthodoxy. But it will not endure the test of time.

More seriously, it will not produce changed lives and it will not prepare people for judgment. Remember, the charge to preach the Word in this way is given in light of the coming judgment (4:1). What is it that will prepare the person whose life is sinful and whose doctrine is erroneous to meet the Judge? Only patient reproval, rebuke and exhortation from the Word. The coming judgment is the reason why we must say the hard things.

Are you doing these things? We all know how easy it is to hold back from saying hard truths from the Word that need to be said. If you are conscious of weakness and failure in this, here is some good news: in God's kindness He gives us the undeserved privilege of fresh opportunities to try again. Today is a new day and this week is a new week. Why not prayerfully resolve, with God's help, to say the hard things when they need to be said as you move forward.

---

1. The Greek verb *parakaleo*, which the NIV translates 'encourage' and the ESV translates 'exhort', means 'to encrouage', yes; but not simply in order to soothe and comfort, but to call to positive action. The translation 'encourage' captures some of the warmth of the Greek word, while 'exhort' captures its urgency. Both are present here, but I would suggest that the context indicates that the emphasis falls on exhortation.

28

Are you being patient with your people?

> Preach the Word; be prepared in season and out of
> season; correct, rebuke and encourage—with great
> patience and careful instruction. (4:2)

I never cease to be amazed how slowly I learn things that others teach me and how slowly others learn things that I teach them. I regularly overestimate my own capacity and the capacity of others to learn. Teaching takes time because learning takes time. We all know that in our heads, but as pastor-teachers we often forget it in practice. Consider for a moment one of the more complicated or difficult doctrines that you know and understand: perhaps the doctrine of the Trinity, or the doctrine of election. How long did it take you to learn and understand and accept that hard doctrine? For me, I reckon it took a number of years in my late teens to understand and accept the doctrine of God's sovereign election. It was both hard to understand and hard to accept. I remember the first occasion when I was conscious of hearing the doctrine of election explained in a sermon. I was about 16, and it really got under my skin. I remember quite clearly going up to my pastor at the end of the sermon and asking for clarification ('Did you *really* mean that?') and then expressing by my quizzical expression my lack of assurance that he had it right. It would be a few years before I would recognise and accept that he was in fact right in what he said.

Now consider the member of your congregation who approaches you at the end of your sermon dealing with the Trinity (or election, or whatever the hard doctrine is) and who questions you or gives you a piece of his mind. How do you react? What do you do? Peter Adam remarks how easily we ourselves can take decades to learn a lesson from the Bible, but then turn around and regard our congregation as stupid if they fail to grasp it on first explanation. How hypocritical we can be! So it is precisely for this reason that Paul reminds Timothy and us who follow to preach with 'complete patience'.

Preaching with 'complete patience' will mean a number of things. It will mean explaining hard truths simply and clearly. It will mean taking the trouble to illustrate our teaching points accurately and engagingly. I take it that doing so is simply a mark of love for our congregation. Preaching with patience will mean repeating ourselves, not simply within a sermon, but being prepared to return to key truths again and again in our preaching programme to drive them home. It will mean taking the time to answer questions that are posed to us during a question time at the end, or over coffee or by email – no matter how unnecessary the question might seem given the wonderful clarity of the sermon we had just preached!

Are you being realistic about how long it will take your people to learn what you teach them? Are you being patient with them? Perhaps we all need to pray that God would graciously remind us of our own slowness to learn and so teach us to be Christ-like in our patience with our people.

29

Are you teaching your people?

> Preach the Word; be prepared in season and out of
> season; correct, rebuke and encourage—with great
> patience and careful instruction. (4:2)

One of the great lessons that evangelical churches throughout
the Western world have been learning over the last couple
of decades is to be mindful of the outsider when organising
services and writing sermons. Many of us have learned to avoid
jargon and insider language, to work hard at our welcome, and
to make clear and unthreatening the way our services function.
We have become used to viewing everything through the eye
of the imaginary unbelieving outsider who could be in our
meetings. All that has been good and fruitful.

However, there is a danger that goes along with becoming
obsessed with the outsider. We can forget that our main weekly
meetings are family gatherings where God's people need to
be fed and 'carefully instructed' from the Word. If we are
always building our meetings around the outsider, the danger
is that we will shy away from much substance in our teaching
for fear of putting off or confusing the non-Christian in our
midst. To some extent, I think there is evidence that this has

been happening in recent years in outward-looking evangelical churches. By and large, sermons have been getting shorter and many preachers are fearful of loading too much doctrinal content or substantial engagement with the text into a Sunday morning slot. I think our strategy has largely been to go light on Sunday mornings and place all our hope into our home groups or growth groups as means of teaching our people. But here in 2 Timothy 4 the charge to teach falls to the pastor-teacher and comes under the banner of preaching. Yes, there will be teaching in other contexts by other people. But Timothy needs to take responsibility for the careful instruction of his people week-by-week through his preaching.

Remember Paul's perspective here. He is about to depart for good. Timothy is now taking up the baton of gospel ministry for the future and is working in a context where there is plenty of false teaching circulating. What does Paul see as the most pressing need for the church as it moves into these uncharted waters of the post-apostolic age? It is the preaching of the Scriptures that contains all the elements of 4:2. If the Christians at Ephesus are to be guarded against false doctrine and so kept in salvation, they need to know the truth and be convinced of it. They need to be *taught*. Timothy must not shy away from teaching them through his preaching (and in other contexts throughout the week, too) for fear of it being too much for them to take. Their defence from error and the future of the gospel depends on him doing it.

Are you really *teaching* your people in your preaching, or are you delegating that responsibility to others and keeping Sundays content-light? Hear Paul's charge again: 'Preach the word...with complete patience *and teaching*.'

30

Are you keeping your head in all situations?

> For the time will come when men will not put
> up with sound doctrine. Instead, to suit their
> own desires, they will gather around them a great
> number of teachers to say what their itching ears
> want to hear. They will turn their ears away from
> the truth and turn aside to myths. But you, *keep your*
> *head in all situations*, endure hardship, do the work
> of an evangelist, discharge all the duties of your
> ministry. (4:3-5)

The rhythm of gospel ministry is punctuated by frequent crises, large and small. Timothy is facing and will face his fair share. It will be a characteristic of 'the last days' (which I take to be this present era; see Acts 2:17 and Heb. 1:2) that people will reject and oppose his message, and false teachers will go about 'deceiving and being deceived' (3:1-9, 13). Paul warns Timothy that people will actually pursue false teachers because they long to hear an easier and less demanding gospel that 'suits their own desires' (4:3). In such a context for ministry, Timothy is going to need to keep his head.

The Ministry Medical

At the very least this will mean Timothy steering 'clear of the heady wine of heretical teaching'.[1] He must be clear about the truth and know it well enough to smell a rat when one comes along. He must be sufficiently enthralled by the truth and delighting in it and feeding on it in his heart that when 'men and women get intoxicated with heady heresies and sparkling novelties'[2] around him he will remain unmoved and will not be drawn in himself. We pastor-teachers need to have a good antenna for heresy, to spot it from a distance, and to remain firmly unimpressed and undazzled by it ourselves. New fads and heresies come along within the evangelical movement with predictable regularity; one retired senior minister said to me recently that he reckons on a major new fad to sweep through evangelicalism every decade, and that seems to be about right to me. Enduring in faithfulness for the long haul will require us to keep our head and remain unmoved when the new fads arrive.

Some of the crises we face in the work of ministry will have less to do with theological movements and more to do with people and groups within our churches. Stories of splits and scandals within our churches are familiar enough. We will, of course, grieve over them, but we must not be shocked or thrown by them. The last days will be marked by seasons when outwardly godly people turn out to be corrupted and do much damage before they are exposed (3:1-9). Some within our churches will not accept the truth we proclaim because they want teachers who will scratch their itching ears and suit their desires (4:3). We must be ready, and we must not be shocked.

This calm, clear-headedness is a characteristic that we need to ask God to cultivate within us. We need to work at this and learn how to manage crises with godliness and self-control. How is my crisis management? How is yours? There is a question here, as well, for those contemplating gospel ministry for the future: Are you someone who can keep your head in a crisis, or are you frankly a bag of nerves? If so, gospel ministry may not be for you.

---

1.   Kelly, *Pastoral*, p. 207.

2.   Stott, *2 Timothy*, p. 112.

31

Are you doing the work of an evangelist?

> But you, keep your head in all situations, endure
> hardship, *do the work of an evangelist,* discharge all the
> duties of your ministry. (4:5)

There are some people who are particularly gifted in evangelism
and are specifically set apart for the work of evangelism (see
Acts 21:8, Eph. 4:11), but there is no clear indication that
Timothy was such a one.[1] Paul is simply instructing him to
get on with the work of evangelism within the context of his
ministry as a pastor-teacher – and the instruction extends to us
as well. There are three areas of our life and ministry we need
to consider here.

The first is our *preaching*. When Paul looks back on his
ministry in Corinth he recalls that he made a conscious decision
to major on one theme in his preaching: 'For I resolved to
know nothing while I was with you except Jesus Christ and
him crucified' (1 Cor. 2:2). If you like, there was one dominant
melodic line to everything he said; all his preaching resonated

---

1 Mounce's insistence that '[t]his is Timothy's spiritual gift to which Paul previously
   referred (1:6; cf. 1 Tim. 1:18)....' (Mounce, *Pastoral*, 576) is speculative and seems
   unjustified.

with the one message of Jesus Christ and Him crucified. That is, Paul majored on the gospel. He told the people week in and week out that Jesus was God's anointed King who had come to be their Saviour through dying in their place and rising again. That is not to say that he said the same thing to them in the same words every week, but each of his sermons proclaimed that same glorious truth from different angles and in different ways. I take it that Jesus Christ and Him crucified is *the* major theme and true melodic line of the whole Bible. In John's gospel Jesus tells us that all of the Old Testament is about Him (John 5:39) and he proceeds to show us as the narrative progresses that the key moment of his ministry (his 'glorification') is his cross and the resurrection that follows. The Bible is all about Jesus and the cross is at the heart of his work. Paul here in 2 Timothy insists that the Old Testament Scriptures 'are able to make you wise for salvation through faith in Christ Jesus' (3:15).

So it follows that any occasion when we expound the Bible and make no mention of Jesus Christ and Him crucified is an occasion when we have missed the point. Faithful preaching of the Word will constantly make clear the message of the cross, and so it will always have an evangelistic edge. That is not to say that every Sunday morning sermon should be a simple evangelistic talk. We need to teach the people in front of us the whole counsel of God. But as we do that we must never move away from the cross, and so our preaching should always have evangelistic value. Although our primary audience is the gathered people of God, we should always work hard to serve the non-Christian as well. Our preaching must be evangelistic.

Next, our *planning* must be evangelistic. That is, we need to be thinking about how we can arrange our church life in order to build in opportunities to work at evangelism as a church family. We need to organise events to which church members can invite non-Christian friends and be confident that they will hear the gospel. It is a very good practice to make a habit of running regular evangelistic courses like 'Christianity Explored', and it is very useful to have particular Sundays set aside as guest events where we deliberately tailor our family gatherings to be evangelistic. And we need to be giving time to train and encourage our people to be effective personal evangelists.

Finally, and most challengingly, we need to work at our own *personal lives* to make sure that we are sharing the gospel with family, friends and neighbours. I hesitate even to write this because I know how poorly I do this myself. It is a tremendous challenge as a pastor-teacher to cultivate and maintain friendships with non-Christians. Church life is busy and many of us have more evening and weekend commitments than we can manage already; for many of us, any spare time is needed for our families. The best way of building links with the community would probably be to join a sports club or a reading group, or something like that, but there hardly seems time. We can only do what we can do; there are only so many hours in the day and days in the week. But we need to be maximising the opportunities we *do* have – with our neighbours, with local businesses (who doesn't go to a barber once in a while …?), with non-Christian family members – and we need to make it a priority for prayer that God would give us opportunities to speak of Jesus. It is very hard to teach and encourage our church family to work hard at evangelism if we hardly do any ourselves.

Are you and I doing the work of an evangelist? What adjustments can we make to our preaching, our church planning, and our personal lives to do that work more effectively?

32

Are you fulfilling your ministry?

> But you, keep your head in all situations, endure
> hardship, do the work of an evangelist, discharge
> all the duties of your ministry. For I am already
> being poured out like a drink offering, and the time
> has come for my departure. I have fought the good
> fight, I have finished the race, I have kept the faith.
> (4:5-7)

Paul was given a specific assignment to be the apostle to the
Gentiles and to take the gospel where it was not yet known. At
the end of his life, having brought the gospel to the heart of
the Roman Empire, he knows that his work is completed. The
Lord has stood by him and upheld him so that through him 'the
message might be fully proclaimed and all the Gentiles might
hear it' (4:17). Paul looks back on his ministry and pictures it as
an athletic contest in the boxing ring and on the running track,
and with joy and gratitude he declares, 'I have fought the good
fight, I have finished the race, I have kept the faith' (4:7).

He says these things to give Timothy a model to follow in
keeping the instruction that comes first: 'discharge all the duties
of your ministry', or 'fulfil your ministry' (ESV). Timothy has

been given a job to do – to preach the Word first at Ephesus and then wherever God sends him. And he is to keep on doing that faithfully and with endurance until he is finished and God moves him on.

You and I will be called to preach the gospel in different situations and places. Within God's sovereign purposes, each of us will have a 'ministry to fulfil'. The instruction here is simply to stick with it in faithfulness and endurance. Keep going until the job is done and God sends you elsewhere. There may be opposition and false teaching around; there almost certainly will be disappointments and trials. Keep going. Do the job God has given you to do. See it through.

This does not mean that we should never move from one ministry post to another; sometimes that is just what we should do. But our focus should be on the task God has given us, and it seems to me that our default assumption should be that we stick with it until God in his sovereignty makes it clear that we are to go elsewhere. Many of us suffer from itchy feet, always looking for a new opportunity and a new challenge. Often, though, the bigger challenge is actually to stay and endure and to keep going in what we are doing. In his kindness, God often blesses long-term ministries with great fruitfulness. As I write I think of one minister here in the UK who is weeks away from retirement after thirty years in one parish. The result? A flourishing local church, yes; and more than that, the map of the U.K. is dotted with faithful Bible-teaching churches, up and down the country, led by men trained under this one minister over the course of three decades invested in one place.

Are you completing the ministry God has given you, or are you constantly looking for the next thing?

33

Are you longing for his appearing?

Now there is in store for me the crown of
righteousness, which the Lord, the righteous Judge,
will award to me on that day—and not only to me,
but also to all who have longed for his appearing.
Do your best to come to me quickly, for Demas,
because he loved this world, has deserted me and
has gone to Thessalonica. (4:8-10)

Here in our ministry health-check Paul draws our attention to
the heart and reminds us of the importance of setting our heart
on the right thing. Actually, the state of the heart has already
been in view in 2 Timothy. The depraved false teachers who
will appear in the terrible times of the last days, Paul has shown
us, will be those who love 'themselves', 'money' and 'pleasure',
but not all that is 'good' or God Himself (3:1-4). Here in 4:8
Paul sets before us the salvation that awaits him and all those
who 'have longed for' (literally, 'have loved') the 'appearing' of
the Lord. Demas, for his part, has deserted Paul because he
'loved this world' (4:10).

The example of Demas is sobering for us. He was one of
Paul's close ministry associates, presumably trained by Paul

himself. He shared in the joys and frustrations of ministry alongside Paul and, we may imagine, showed promise as a leader of the church beyond Paul's day. But the social and political cost of ministering alongside an incarcerated apostle was too high for Demas. Perhaps he saw that he could go the same way as Paul if he did not watch out. So, he deserted Paul and made his way to Thessalonica.

The really scary thing about Demas, though, is that there is no indication here that he left ministry and went back to another kind of work. All we know is that he abandoned Paul because he loved his comfort and security in this world too much to share in suffering alongside Paul. It may well be that Demas found a more appealing ministry role in Thessalonica where things were a bit more stable.[1] Perhaps he sensed an overwhelming 'call' to ministry in a quieter and more receptive place. Demas is scary because, in our present day, he may well be the sort of minister who is committed to evangelical doctrine, is a powerful Bible preacher, attends evangelical ministry conferences and buys books like this one. To all outward appearances, he may be much like you and me. But he has actually cast his lot in with this world, has not set his love upon that future appearing of the Lord Jesus, and so is unwilling to give himself to costly, self-sacrificial ministry. There is probably something of Demas in most of us.

So we need to examine our hearts for a moment. Where is our true love set? Does the prospect of Jesus' great appearing thrill our hearts and fill our horizons? Are we longing for his appearing to such an extent that we will willingly suffer in this present world for the sake of his name? Or is our love *really* set on our comfort and security and respectability in the here and now? We will know that it is if we find ourselves putting distance between ourselves and fellow ministers who are embarrassingly clear and outspoken in their defence of the truth in our local area or denomination. We will know that our

---

1.   As Kelly suggests; *Pastoral,* p. 213.

love is on this present world if we find ourselves planning our next ministry move with an eye on how straightforward the job will be and how comfortable the situation. Or is our love set on the Lord Jesus and his appearing? We will know that it is if we find ourselves willing to endure disgrace for His sake and inconvenience on His account, and if we find ourselves gladly partnering with those whom the world derides.

34

Are you a bookworm?

> When you come, bring the cloak that I left with
> Carpus at Troas, and my scrolls, especially the
> parchments. (4:13)

Picture Paul in a cold and wet Roman prison, arms in shackles, unable to sleep for lack of bed or comfort, probably unable to wash and almost certainly short on food. What does he long to have with him? A warmer cloak (fair enough), his scrolls, and above all, the parchments. Possibly the parchments are Paul's copies of his Greek Old Testament and his scrolls are perhaps his commentaries or collected sayings of Jesus. Whatever his book collection contained, the very fact that he wanted them so badly while his mind might well have been focused elsewhere gives us a window into the heartbeat of his ministry. Paul was a man of books. He invested time and energy in his study. His evangelisation of the Gentile world was founded fundamentally, not on charisma or mere strategy, but on a thorough knowledge of God's Word. The engine room of Paul's ministry was his study. We see the full fruit of his knowledge of the Scriptures in books like Romans and Ephesians, but it undergirded his whole ministry.

The Ministry Medical

Do we take seriously the priority of knowing the Bible and spending real time in study? Is the hard work of deepening your understanding and knowledge of the Word fundamental to your ministry, or is it sidelined? If it has been fundamental, does it remain so? In part, this question boils down to practicalities. Are you being given the time for reading and reflection that you need, and are you preserving that time? Your church leadership team will not instinctively understand the substantial time needed for grappling with the Bible and its application to the present day. It may simply not have occurred to them, and so may be down to you to tell them and to encourage them to set you free for it. If you do not have the time to give to the Word, your preaching ministry will run threadbare and the church will sooner or later feel the cost of that.

But once we are given the time, we then need to give ourselves – and keep on giving ourselves – to the hard work of grappling with the Bible itself and reading books that will help us know it better. If you feel like you are running on empty in your preaching ministry at the moment, this may be the reason: you have stopped spending time deepening your knowledge of the Bible, and you are simply recycling insights that you picked up back at college (or from your favourite online preacher). But Paul, the great apostle and author of much of the New Testament, finds at the end of his life and ministry that there is more to discover in the Word, and he is desperate to get his hands on his books. Do you and I share that longing and priority?

If you are reading this as someone contemplating gospel ministry for the future, it is worthwhile to pause and consider whether you have the capacity for serious and sustained study. You may have a passion for the gospel and gifts in handling people and a godly life, but if you hate the thought of hours spent in study of the Word, the office of pastor-teacher is probably not for you.

35

Are you a strategist?

Do your best to come to me quickly, for
Demas, because he loved this world, has
deserted me and has gone to Thessalonica.
Crescens has gone to Galatia, and Titus to
Dalmatia. Only Luke is with me. Get Mark and
bring him with you, because he is helpful to
me in my ministry. I sent Tychicus to Ephesus.
(4:9-12)

Greet Priscilla and Aquila and the household
of Onesiphorus. Erastus stayed in Corinth, and
I left Trophimus sick in Miletus. Do your best
to get here before winter. Eubulus greets you,
and so do Pudens, Linus, Claudia and all the
brothers (4:19-21).

We tend to picture Paul as a lone ranger going off on a solo
mission to evangelise the Mediterranean rim with no backup
and no help. But if we take note of the list of names at the end
of his letters the ministry associates mentioned at other points

in his letters and in Acts, we come up with a list of 100 people or so with whom Paul was working.[1]

For three years I worked as a school teacher at the school in London where Field Marshal Montgomery, a hero of the Second World War, was a pupil. Montgomery used a room in the old school building to plan details of the D-Day invasion of France in 1944, and one of the school's great treasures is a huge map of Europe that Montgomery used to plan his troop deployments for that great endeavour. Paul here in prison has a map of the Mediterranean rim in his mind and he has in his view all the members of his team and their movements. He has been doing for many years what he instructed Timothy to do in 2:2 – he has been training and discipling others to carry on the work of the gospel.

We have just been thinking about the fact that Paul spent time in his books, and so he did; but he was no hermit. He was interested in people and he was thinking strategy all the time. 'Who needs to be where in order to cover the needs of gospel ministry in a given place?' 'Who do I need here to help me?' Mark, he reckons, is vital to his own ministry in Rome (limited as it was by imprisonment!). Tychicus would be needed in Ephesus now that Paul was asking Timothy to leave there and join him in Rome. And on it goes. The point is that Paul had a big picture strategy and he knew that the placement of the right people in key areas was essential. So he gave thought to it and was happy to give leadership to others in that way.

Our situations in ministry will all be different; we will have varying levels of responsibility and oversight of others, and the size of our geographical horizons will vary hugely. But if we are in the role of pastor-teacher, we must think strategically and in terms of building and deploying a team. We must be realistic about the fact that we ourselves will not be around forever,

---

1. Of course, of these 100 people, some would be more closely and permanently associated with Paul than others. For a further discussion, see E. Earle Ellis, 'Paul and his co-workers,' *New Testament Studies* 17 (1971): pp. 437-52. I am grateful to Paul Barnett for his help in pursuing this line of enquiry and for pointing me to Ellis' article.

and even while we are around, we are not able to do everything ourselves.

Maybe this kind of strategic thinking will involve getting a map of your parish or the area for which your church is the only reachable evangelical church and putting that map up in your study. Where is the next home group or growth group needed? Who could be trained up to run it? Where, perhaps, should you be thinking about a church plant? Who are the key people and the key families who could go? Who could be the elders, and who the pastor-teacher?

Are you thinking strategically and building a team, or are you in maintenance (or worse, survival) mode? Even in prison and facing death, Paul was thinking strategy, team building, and gospel growth.

36

Are you zealous for the Lord's glory?

> But the Lord stood at my side and gave me
> strength, so that *through me the message might be fully
> proclaimed* and all the Gentiles might hear it. And
> I was delivered from the lion's mouth. The Lord
> will rescue me from every evil attack and will bring
> me safely to his heavenly kingdom. *To him be glory
> for ever* and ever. Amen. (4:17-18)

There is a structural temptation in ministry toward pride and self-congratulation. Our key work of preaching is public and if we do it well we often receive gratitude and commendation. It is very easy for us to enjoy that rather too much and to pursue the praise of others and the increase of our reputation. God in his kindness often sends people and situations (sometimes very painful ones) to humble us. But we do well to note Paul's own mindset and to take it as our model.

Notice, first, Paul's self-understanding. Here at the end of his ministry, Paul could feel inclined to be rather pleased with himself. He has endured the trial of prison (probably for the second time now) and has not only remained faithful to Jesus, but is still thinking actively about gospel proclamation and gospel growth, even as he faces imminent death. While there was no one to stand with him at his first trial (4:16), the Lord helped him, and it seems that Paul may even have taken the opportunity at his trial to proclaim the gospel. What is striking is the way Paul describes his part in all this: '...the Lord stood at my side and gave me strength, so that *through me the message might be fully proclaimed*....' Paul was weak in and of himself, but the Lord gave him strength. Paul probably had no idea what to say, but the Lord's purpose was that 'through' Paul the message might be proclaimed. Paul was only a conduit for the Lord's proclamation of the message. He was no hero for continuing to preach the gospel under such trial. How do you and I see ourselves, as heroes or as conduits?

Notice, next, the ground of Paul's confidence. When Paul stood trial at Rome there was no one there to provide backup and testify on his behalf. Paul could have turned to self-sufficiency at this point; he was an intelligent man with a gift for articulate and persuasive speech. Perhaps, in the absence of friends to help, he could simply have talked his way out of this one. In human terms, he may have done just that. We do not know what he said at that first trial, but something obviously worked. But, for Paul, his deliverance from immediate execution on that occasion was not down to himself and his own gifts; no, '...the Lord stood at my side and gave me strength....And I was delivered....', and, more than that, 'The Lord will rescue me from every evil attack and will bring me safely to his heavenly kingdom' (4:17-18). Paul knew that he was weak and vulnerable, but the Lord was strong. It may have been that the Lord exercised his strength through Paul, but it was the Lord's strength and not Paul's. If ministry is going well and we are enjoying outward success and the praise of men, do we still believe that we are weak and our only security is in the fact that the Lord is strong?

Finally, notice Paul's driving ambition: 'To him be glory for ever and ever.' It is so easy to seek our own glory and the increase of our own reputation, and gospel ministry is as easy a place to do that as any. Because our sinful nature is naturally proud and self-centred, we will have to battle against this and live a life of ongoing repentance in this area. Alongside that, we need to make sure that we are captured by Paul's vision for God's glory. Paul knew that the reputation of God was the most important thing in the universe. He recognised that God is entirely glorious, so there is no greater pursuit than to make that glory known and to reflect that glory in his own life and ministry. The glory of God is the thing of absolute value and undiminishing worth. If we can see, with Paul, that God's reputation is all-important, we will learn to spend ourselves in service of his reputation and not our own. What is our driving ambition; what do we hope to achieve in our ministry? Is it the increase of our own glory, or the increase of the Lord's? May the Lord teach us to pray with all our heart, 'To him be the glory for ever and ever'.

Bibliography

Adam, Peter. *2 Timothy – The Making of the Man of God.* Addresses given at the *Proclamation Trust Senior Ministers' Conference*, 2001. Online: www.proctrust.org.uk.

Fee, Gordon D. *1 and 2 Timothy, Titus. New International Biblical Commentary.* (Milton Keynes, UK: Paternoster, 1984.)

Green, Christopher. *Finishing the Race: Reading 2 Timothy Today.* (Sydney, Australia: Aquila Press, 2000.)

Hughes, R. Kent and Bryan Chapell. *1-2 Timothy and Titus: To Guard the Deposit. Preaching the Word.* (Wheaton, USA: Crossway, 2012.)

Kelly, J.N.D. *The Pastoral Epistles: I&II Timothy Titus. Black's New Testament Commentaries.* (London, UK: A&C Black, 1963.)

Lucas, R.C. *2 Timothy.* Addresses given at the *Proclamation Trust Evangelical Ministry Assembly*, 1986. Online: www.proctrust. org.uk.

Mounce, William D. *Pastoral Epistles. Word Biblical Commentary 46.* (Nashville, USA: Thomas Nelson, 2000.)

Stott, John R.W. *I Believe in Preaching*. (London, UK: Hodder and Stoughton, 1982.)

_____ *The Message of 2 Timothy: Guard the gospel. The Bible Speaks Today.* (Nottingham, UK: Inter-Varsity Press, 1973.)

PT Resources

RESOURCES FOR PREACHERS AND BIBLE TEACHERS

PT Resources, a ministry of The Proclamation Trust, provides a range of multimedia resources for preachers and Bible teachers.

Teach the Bible Series (Christian Focus & PT Resources)

The Teaching the Bible Series, published jointly with *Christian Focus Publications*, is written by preachers, for preachers, and is specifically geared to the purpose of God's Word – its proclamation as living truth. Books in the series aim to help the reader move beyond simply understanding a text to communicating and applying it.

Current titles include: *Teaching 1 Peter, Teaching 1 Timothy, Teaching Acts, Teaching Amos, Teaching Ephesians, Teaching Isaiah, Teaching John, Teaching Matthew, Teaching Numbers, Teaching Romans, Teaching the Christian Hope* and *Spirit of Truth*.

Forthcoming titles include: *Teaching Daniel, Teaching 1 and 2 Kings* and *Teaching Nehemiah*.

The Ministry Medical

Practical Preacher series

PT Resources publish a number of books addressing practical issues for preachers. These include *The Priority of Preaching, Bible Delight, Hearing the Spirit* and *The Ministry Medical*. Forthcoming titles include a ministry checklist based on the book of 2 Timothy.

Online resources

We publish a large number of audio resources online, all of which are free to download. These are searchable through our website by speaker, date, topic and Bible book. The resources include:

- sermon series; examples of great preaching which not only demonstrate faithful principles but which will refresh and encourage the heart of the preacher

- instructions; audio which helps the teacher or preacher understand, open up and teach individual books of the Bible by getting to grips with their central message and purpose

- conference recordings; audio from all our conferences including the annual Evangelical Ministry Assembly. These talks discuss ministry and preaching issues.

An increasing number of resources are also available in video download form.

Online DVD

PT Resources have recently published online our collection of instructional videos by David Jackman. This material has been taught over the past 20 years on our PT Cornhill training course and around the world. it gives step by step instructions on handling each genre of biblical literature.

There is also an online workbook. The videos are suitable for preachers and those teaching the Bible in a variety of different contexts. Access to all the videos is free of charge.

The Proclaimer

Visit the Proclaimer blog for regular updates on matters to do with preaching. This is a short, punchy blog refreshed daily which is written by preachers and for preachers. It can be accessed via the PT website or through www. theproclaimer.org.uk.

'Teaching' titles from
Christian Focus and PT Resources

Teaching Numbers
ISBN 978-1-78191-156-3

Teaching Isaiah
ISBN 978-1-84550-565-3

Teaching Daniel
ISBN 978-1-84550-457-1
(Summer 2014)

Teaching Amos
ISBN 978-1-84550-142-6

Teaching Matthew
ISBN 978-1-84550-480-9

Teaching John
ISBN 978-1-85792-790-0

Teaching Acts
ISBN 978-1-84550-255-3

Teaching Romans
(volume 1)
ISBN 978-1-84550-455-7

Teaching Romans
(volume 2)
ISBN 978-1-84550-456-4

Teaching Ephesians
ISBN 978-1-84550-684-1

Teaching 1 Timothy
ISBN 978-1-84550-808-1

Teaching 1 Peter
ISBN 978-1-84550-347-5

Teaching the Christian Hope
ISBN 978-1-85792-518-0

Spirit of Truth
ISBN 978-1-84550-057-3

About the Proclamation Trust

We exist to promote church-based expository Bible ministry and especially to equip and encourage Biblical expository preachers because we recognise the primary role of preaching in God's sovereign purposes in the world through the local church.

Biblical (the message)
We believe the Bible is God's written Word and that, by the work of the Holy Spirit, as it is faithfully preached God's voice is truly heard.

Expository (the method)
Central to the preacher's task is correctly handling the Bible, seeking to discern the mind of the Spirit in the passage being expounded through prayerful study of the text in the light of its context in the biblical book and the Bible as a whole. This divine message must then be preached in dependence on the Holy Spirit to the minds, hearts and wills of the contemporary hearers.

Preachers (the messengers)
The public proclamation of God's Word by suitably gifted leaders is fundamental to a ministry that honours God, builds the church and reaches the world. God uses weak jars of clay in this task who need encouragement to persevere in their biblical convictions, ministry of God's Word and godly walk with Christ.

We achieve this through:

- PT Cornhill: a one year full-time or two-year part-time church based training course

- PT Conferences: offering practical encouragement for Bible preachers, teachers and ministers' wives

- PT Resources: including books, online resources, the PT blog (www.theproclaimer.org.uk) and podcasts

Christian Focus Publications

Our mission statement –

STAYING FAITHFUL

In dependence upon God we seek to impact the world through literature faithful to His infallible Word, the Bible. Our aim is to ensure that the Lord Jesus Christ is presented as the only hope to obtain forgiveness of sin, live a useful life and look forward to heaven with Him.

Our books are published in four imprints:

CHRISTIAN
FOCUS

Popular works including biographies, commentaries, basic doctrine and Christian living.

CHRISTIAN
HERITAGE

Books representing some of the best material from the rich heritage of the church.

MENTOR

Books written at a level suitable for Bible College and seminary students, pastors, and other serious readers. The imprint includes commentaries, doctrinal studies, examination of current issues and church history.

CF4•K

Children's books for quality Bible teaching and for all age groups: Sunday school curriculum, puzzle and activity books; personal and family devotional titles, biographies and inspirational stories – because you are never too young to know Jesus!

Christian Focus Publications Ltd,
Geanies House, Fearn, Ross-shire,
IV20 1TW, Scotland, United Kingdom.
www.christianfocus.com